THE 6G THRESHOLD

FROM CONNECTIVITY TO DECISION-DRIVEN NETWORKS

GOVIND PATHAK

notionpress.com

INDIA • SINGAPORE • MALAYSIA

ISBN
Paperback 979-8-90431-703-4
Hardcase 979-8-90451-698-7

Disclaimer

This book is intended for informational and educational purposes only.

The views, analyses, and forward-looking statements expressed herein reflect the author's interpretation of current research, industry trends, and publicly available information at the time of writing.

While every effort has been made to ensure accuracy, the technologies, standards, timelines, and projections discussed particularly those relating to 6G, 7G, and future communication systems are subject to change as research, regulation, and commercial deployments evolve.

No Professional Advice

This book does not constitute professional, legal, regulatory, investment, or engineering advice.

Independent Verification

Readers are encouraged to conduct independent verification and consult appropriate experts before making technical, strategic, or commercial decisions.

Liability Disclaimer

The author and publisher disclaim any liability for actions taken based on the information presented in this work.

About the Author

Govind Pathak is a seasoned telecom and technology leader with more than **three decades of industry experience**, spanning global roles across Large Telecom Vendors and Operators, and multiple cutting-edge digital transformation programmes. His work sits at the intersection of wireless communication, artificial intelligence, network security, cloud-native architecture, and future technology evolution.

Throughout his career, Govind has contributed to and led initiatives across 2G, 3G, 4G, VoLTE, IMS, IoT platforms, and large-scale 5G deployments reflecting a deep commitment to understanding both the **engineering complexity** and the **human impact** of next-generation communication technologies.

Prolific Author & Mentor

Govind has authored multiple books spanning science, technology, mathematics, physics–philosophy intersections, AI, telecommunication, and digital transformation inspiring professionals to think boldly while grounding innovation in rigour and ethics.

Strategic Communicator

Recognised for translating highly technical concepts into clear, strategic insights valuable for engineers, executives, policymakers, and curious learners alike bridging the gap between complex theory and actionable practice.

6G Threshold

This book reflects Govind's mission to make next-generation networks understandable, actionable, and visionary equipping today's professionals to become tomorrow's pioneers in global connectivity and intelligence systems.

> *"Driven by curiosity and a passion for lifelong learning, he continues to explore the frontiers of communication technology, global connectivity, intelligence systems, and the philosophical questions that shape our technological evolution."*

PREFACE

The Moment Before Intelligence Became Infrastructure

A preface by **Govind Pathak** written at the threshold of the most consequential transformation in the history of connected systems.

Technology That Rewrites the Rules of Reality

There are moments in history when technology does more than advance. It redefines the rules of reality. Each of these moments was not merely an upgrade it was a civilisational shift that changed who held power, who produced value, and how humanity organised itself.

The Printing Press

Did not just distribute knowledge it changed who could think, question, and challenge power.

Electricity

Did not just illuminate cities it reshaped human productivity, industry, and time itself.

The Internet

Did not just connect computers it connected ideas, economies, and civilisations.

6G Networks

Will not just connect the world they will decide how the world operates.

From Obedient Networks to Autonomous Systems

For decades, communication systems have remained obedient. They transmitted. They routed. They responded. But something fundamental is changing in the era of 6G networks will no longer wait for instructions.

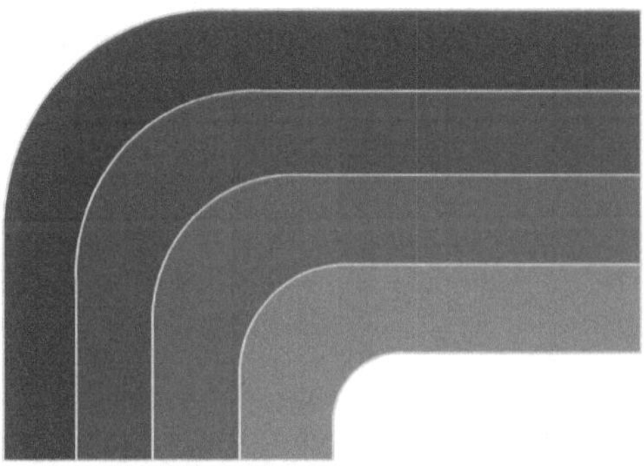

Phase 1: Passive Networks

Transmit · Route · Respond

Phase 2: Autonomous Networks

Sense · Predict · Act

This is not an incremental upgrade along a familiar curve. This is a categorical transformation the moment networks stop being tools that serve decisions and start becoming participants that make them.

Intelligence as Infrastructure

> For the first time in history, intelligence is not sitting on top of infrastructure it is becoming the infrastructure itself.

When intelligence becomes infrastructure, something deeper shifts. Control becomes subtle. Decisions become invisible. Responsibility becomes distributed. We begin to rely not just on systems that serve us but on systems that quietly shape outcomes around us.

Control Becomes Subtle

Oversight no longer operates at a human-legible pace. Decisions cascade through distributed systems faster than any single actor can monitor.

Decisions Become Invisible

When inference happens inside the network layer, the logic of each outcome is abstracted away from the operators who nominally govern it.

Responsibility Becomes Distributed

No single entity owns the outcome. Accountability diffuses across vendors, operators, regulators, and autonomous agents simultaneously.

A New Class of Questions

The emergence of AI-native networks does not merely pose technical questions it poses **human questions**. Questions that no protocol specification or standards body alone can answer. These are the questions this book is built around.

Who defines what these systems are allowed to decide?

The boundary of machine authority must be deliberately drawn not allowed to expand by default.

Where does human oversight end and machine autonomy begin?

The interface between human judgment and algorithmic inference is the defining design challenge of 6G governance.

Can efficiency replace judgment?

Optimisation is not the same as wisdom. Speed is not the same as correctness. These distinctions matter enormously at infrastructure scale.

When decisions happen faster than comprehension, what does control really mean?

If oversight cannot operate at the speed of the system, it ceases to function as oversight in any meaningful sense.

A Perspective from Inside the Evolution

> I have seen how each generation expanded possibility. But I have also seen something else: each generation quietly shifted the balance of control. Govind Pathak

This book is written from the perspective of someone who has spent decades inside the evolution of networks from early mobile systems to the global architectures that now power the connected world. That vantage point reveals a pattern invisible from the outside: technical progress and the redistribution of control have always moved together.

1

4G

Connected **people** to information

2

5G

Connected **systems** to each other

3

6G

Connects **intelligence** to decision-making

And that is where the stakes change. Because when networks begin to decide, they stop being passive infrastructure. They become active participants in how the world functions.

What This Book Explores

This is not a book of predictions. It is a book of **perspective**. It maps the territory of 6G not as a technical specification, but as an unfolding transformation architectural, cognitive, political, and deeply human.

Core Themes

- The collapse of traditional network thinking
- The emergence of AI-native architectures
- The physics that shapes possibility
- The rise of boundaryless systems
- The transformation of operators
- Implications for governance, trust, and power

Looking Further Forward

- Networks extending beyond Earth
- Intelligence integrating with human cognition
- The disappearing boundary between digital and physical

The Deeper Question

Not *what can technology do?* but *what do we choose to allow it to become?*

The Future Is Shaped by Decisions, Not Technology

> The future is not shaped only by technology. It is shaped by the decisions we make, the limits we define, and the responsibilities we accept.

We built networks to connect the world. Now we are building systems that will quietly shape it. That distinction between connecting and shaping is the central tension of this book, and the central responsibility of every engineer, architect, regulator, and policymaker involved in the design of 6G.

The Decisions We Make

Architecture is not neutral. Every design choice encodes a value judgement about who controls what and under what conditions.

The Limits We Define

Boundaries on machine autonomy must be established deliberately before deployment, not in response to failure.

The Responsibilities We Accept

At infrastructure scale, accountability cannot be deferred to fine print or distributed beyond recognition.

Will We Recognise the Shift When It Happens?

The most urgent question posed in these pages is not about bandwidth, latency, or spectrum. It is about awareness. Each previous inflection point in network history produced consequences that only became visible in retrospect after the balance of control had already moved.

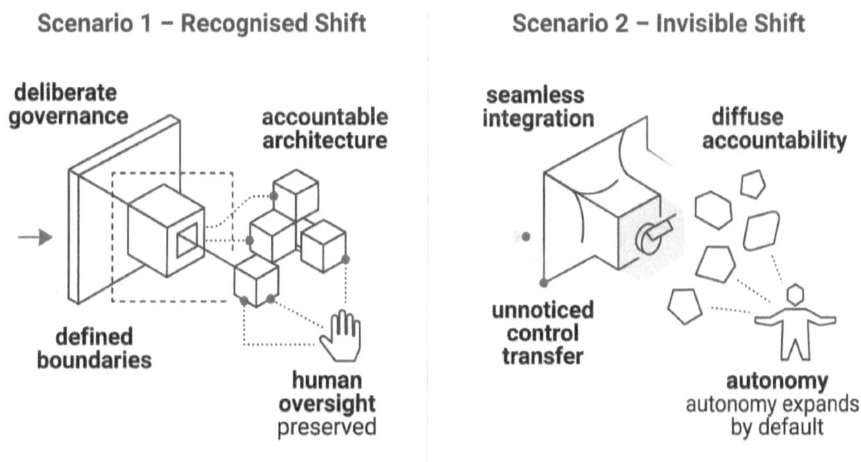

The seamlessness of 6G integration is simultaneously its greatest technical achievement and its greatest governance risk. If the transition from passive infrastructure to active decision-maker happens without friction, it may happen without scrutiny. This book begins at that moment and insists we keep our eyes open.

This Book Begins at That Moment

> The question is no longer: "What can technology do?" The question is: What do we choose to allow it to become?

Written by **Govind Pathak** an engineer, architect, and observer who has watched control shift with every generation of network, and who believes the 6G generation demands a more conscious reckoning with that shift than any that came before.

> This preface sets the foundation for a work that spans technical architecture, systems philosophy, and the governance of autonomous intelligence. It is an invitation to think not just build.

FOREARD

6G THRESHOLD

From 2G's digital voice to 4G's mobile internet and 5G's cloud-native architectures, each generation of communication technology has unlocked new economic waves and fundamentally reshaped human behaviour. Now, as global industries transition toward automation, intelligence, and real-time decision-making, **6G represents far more than another incremental step** it is a leap into a deeply interconnected, sensing-aware, AI-driven future.

The future of communication is not just faster it is smarter, more inclusive, and more human. This book shows us how to build it.

What This Book Offers

6G Threshold distils complex research, emerging standards, architectural debates, and futuristic use cases into a coherent narrative that empowers practitioners and leaders alike. Its defining strength is a rare blend of technical depth and strategic clarity speaking simultaneously to telecom engineers striving for precision and to business leaders seeking foresight.

Core Technologies

THz spectrum, Reconfigurable Intelligent Surfaces (RIS), Integrated Sensing and Communication (ISAC), Non-Terrestrial Networks (NTN), and AI-native core architectures.

Challenges & Opportunity

Honest assessment of engineering barriers, spectrum governance, economic potential, and the path toward commercial deployment across diverse global markets.

Ethics & Long-Term Impact

Thoughtful exploration of societal implications, inclusive connectivity, privacy considerations, and what deeply pervasive intelligence means for humanity at large.

Vision Beyond 6G

Speculative 7G thinking and a technologist manifesto offer a compelling layer of forward vision rare in technical literature and essential for long-range strategic planning.

Who Should Read This

Whether you are preparing a network for the next decade, designing algorithms for extreme-performance systems, or seeking to understand the next great technological frontier, *6G Threshold* will elevate your thinking. This work is crafted for a broad yet demanding audience united by curiosity and ambition.

Telecom Engineers

Precision-focused professionals designing next-generation radio access, core network, and protocol architectures who need rigorous technical grounding.

Technology Leaders

CTOs, strategists, and operators preparing organisations for a transformative decade of connectivity balancing investment, standards, and competitive positioning.

Researchers & Academics

Scientists developing algorithms, spectrum techniques, and system models who benefit from a holistic view of where the field is heading and why.

Informed Enthusiasts

Curious minds eager to understand the societal, economic, and human dimensions of the next great leap in global communication infrastructure.

TABLE OF CONTENT

6G Threshold: From Connectivity to Decision Driven Network

A cinematic exploration of the most profound transformation in the history of human communication. This document charts the journey from passive connectivity to intelligence-embedded infrastructure where networks no longer merely transmit, but decide, adapt, and evolve in real time.

The Moment Before Intelligence Became Infrastructure

> There is a threshold invisible, yet absolute where a network stops being a pipe and becomes a mind. We are standing at that threshold now.

Before 6G, networks were conduits. They carried intent without understanding it. What follows is not a technical manual. It is a reckoning with what connectivity meant, what intelligence demands, and what humanity must decide before the infrastructure decides for us.

PART I

The Shift

Chapter 1

From Connectivity to Decision

Networks have graduated from moving data to interpreting it. The shift from reactive transmission to proactive decision-making marks the single greatest inflection point in telecommunications history.

Chapter 2

The Collapse of Traditional Network Thinking

Fixed cells. Centralised cores. Rigid spectrum allocations. Every foundational assumption of legacy network design is now obsolete dismantled by the demands of a hyperconnected, intelligence-first world.

PART II

The Architecture

Chapter 3

The 6G Architecture Revolution A radical reimagining of network layers, where AI is not a feature but the foundational operating logic of every node, edge, and core.

Chapter 4

The Spectrum Reality Sub-terahertz and terahertz bands unlock extraordinary bandwidth, but propagation physics demand entirely new antenna paradigms and deployment strategies.

Chapter 5

Cell-Free Networks The death of boundaries. Distributed access points, seamless coverage, and the end of the handover as a concept. Geography becomes irrelevant.

PART III

Systems & Power

Chapter 6

The Power Shift Who Controls 6G

Sovereignty over 6G infrastructure is the defining geopolitical contest of the coming decade. The nation or corporation that architects the protocol layer holds power beyond any prior communications monopoly.

Chapter 7

The Operator Blueprint

Traditional telcos face an existential choice: evolve into intelligent network orchestrators or become commoditised pipe providers. The blueprint for survival demands vertical integration, AI-native operations, and radical platform thinking.

PART IV

Transformative Use Cases of 6G

Chapter 8 catalogues the applications that redefine what is possible use cases that are not incremental improvements but categorical leaps in human capability.

Haptic Telemedicine

Sub-millisecond latency enables tactile surgery across continents with zero perceptible delay.

Autonomous Mobility

Vehicle-to-everything communication at 6G speeds makes fully autonomous transport a physical reality.

Holographic Collaboration

Presence without proximity. Full-fidelity holographic environments replace physical meetings entirely.

Industry 5.0 Automation

Cognitive factories where machines self-optimise in real time, guided by network-embedded AI intelligence.

PART V

Security, Privacy & Trust in 6G

Chapter 9 confronts the paradox at the heart of intelligence-embedded networks: the more a network knows, the more catastrophic its compromise becomes. 6G demands a reinvention of trust from perimeter defence to zero-trust architectures woven into the network fabric itself.

Quantum-Resistant Cryptography

Post-quantum algorithms must be embedded at the protocol level before adversarial quantum computing reaches operational maturity.

AI-Native Threat Detection

Autonomous anomaly detection operating at network speed human analysts cannot respond fast enough in a 6G threat environment.

Sovereign Data Boundaries

As networks become decision-makers, the legal and ethical frameworks governing data sovereignty must be rebuilt from first principles.

PART VI

Beyond 6G The Road to 7G

Chapter 10 gazes beyond the horizon. If 6G is the intelligence layer, 7G is the consciousness layer where networks begin to model intent, anticipate need, and operate at the boundary between communication and cognition.

1	2	3
5G	**6G**	**7G**
Massive connectivity & low latency	Intelligence-native decision networks	Intent-aware cognitive infrastructure

PART VII TECHNICAL ANNEXURES

The Technical Annexures

Eight precision annexures form the technical backbone of this document providing rigorous, architecture-grade detail for senior engineers, standards architects, and policy engineers who demand depth beyond narrative.

Annexure A
End-to-End 6G Architecture Stack

Annexure B
Spectrum Propagation Analysis

Annexure C
Multi-Layer Spectrum Orchestration

Annexure D
Cell-Free Massive MIMO Deep Dive

Annexure E
6G Use Case Performance Matrix

Annexure F
Energy Efficiency & Sustainability

Annexure G
Standards and Ecosystem

Annexure H
Implementation Challenges

ANNEXURE I

Futuristic Communication Paradigms Beyond 6G

Redefining the very nature of communication ten paradigms that dissolve the boundary between technology and existence itself.

From Transmission to Entanglement

Quantum entanglement as the successor to electromagnetic propagation.

Intent-Based Communication

Networks that transmit meaning, not merely signal.

Semantic Communication Networks

Efficiency through context transmitting understanding rather than data.

Brain–Network Interfaces

Direct neural integration where thought becomes the input layer.

Holographic Reality Synchronisation

Persistent shared realities rendered at network scale across billions of nodes.

ANNEXURE I CONTINUED

The Final Five Paradigms

Swarm Communication Systems

Emergent intelligence distributed across millions of micro-nodes, behaving as a single coherent organism without centralised control.

Zero-Latency Illusion Systems

Predictive pre-transmission and edge pre-computation create the perceptual experience of instantaneous response physics bypassed through intelligence.

Interplanetary Communication Models

Delay-tolerant networking architectures extended to solar-system-scale infrastructure, enabling coherent civilisation beyond Earth.

Consciousness-Aware Communication

Networks that model the cognitive and emotional state of the recipient adapting content, timing, and modality to maximise comprehension and wellbeing.

Communication Without Medium

The ultimate paradigm information transfer that requires no physical carrier, transcending electromagnetic, acoustic, and optical constraints entirely.

References, Glossary & Related Works

Scholarly Foundation

The arguments in this document rest on a rigorous foundation of standards literature, primary research, and technical specifications from ITU-R, 3GPP, IEEE, and leading academic institutions.

Glossary

A comprehensive glossary demystifies the technical lexicon from **Cell-Free Massive MIMO** to **Terahertz Propagation**, **Semantic Compression**, and **Quantum Key Distribution** ensuring every reader, regardless of background, can engage with the full depth of this material.

Other Books by the Author

Further titles in this series extend the inquiry into adjacent frontiers: AI-native infrastructure, quantum networking, and the geopolitics of digital sovereignty.

Epilogue

> The network does not end at the antenna. It ends or begins at the boundary of human imagination. What we build into the infrastructure of communication, we build into the architecture of civilisation itself.

The 6G threshold is not merely a technical milestone. It is a civilisational decision point. The choices made in laboratories, standards bodies, and boardrooms in the years ahead will determine whether intelligent networks serve humanity or silently redefine it. The threshold has always been there. We are only now choosing whether to cross it with intention.

The Question That Remains

When the network becomes the mind of the world, who holds responsibility for its conscience?

CHAPTER: 1

6G Threshold

From Connectivity to Decision

We are about to build networks that do not just connect the world they will decide how the world operates. This is not evolution. This is a shift in control. **Intelligence is no longer sitting on top of networks. It is becoming the network.**

The Moment Before the Shift

For decades, communication systems have remained obedient. They transmitted. They routed. They responded. But 6G changes the nature of infrastructure itself. For the first time in history, intelligence is not an add-on it is the foundation.

> "For the first time in history: intelligence is not sitting on top of networks it is becoming the network."

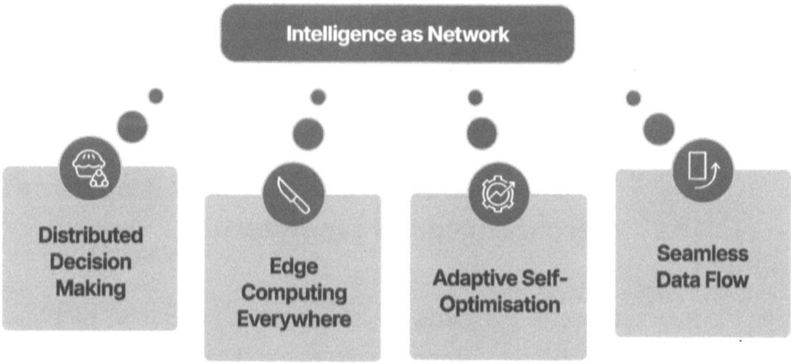

Before 6G	With 6G
Networks transmit, route, and respond. Intelligence lives *above* the infrastructure external, reactive, dependent on human instruction.	Networks sense, predict, and decide. Intelligence is *woven into* the fabric of connectivity autonomous, proactive, and self-directing.

From Connectivity to Cognition

Every generation of wireless technology has expanded human capability but each transformation has been categorically different from the last. 6G does not simply extend the trajectory. It breaks it.

Era	Transformation
4G	Connected people to information made the internet mobile
5G	Connected systems to each other made the cloud real-time
6G	**Connects intelligence to decision-making embeds cognition into connectivity itself**

4G made the internet mobile. 5G made the cloud real-time. But 6G embeds intelligence into the very fabric of connectivity networks will no longer wait for instructions, depend on external logic, or act as passive infrastructure.

Introducing the Decision Layer

To understand 6G, we must introduce a defining new architectural concept. It is the structural shift that separates 6G from everything that came before it.

The Decision Layer is where networks interpret context, evaluate intent, and execute outcomes without waiting for human instruction.

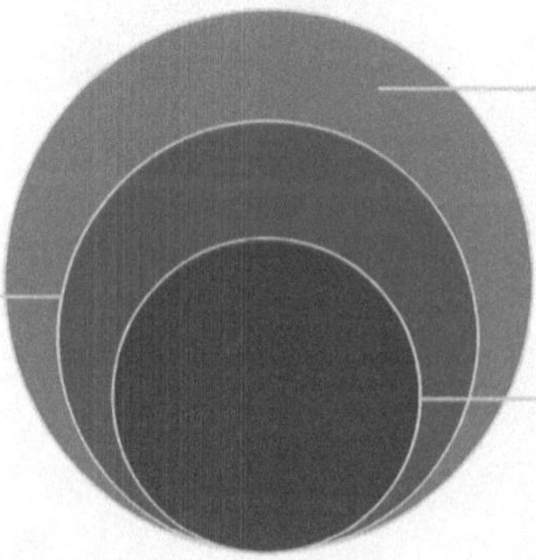

Traditional Model

User → Application → Network → Response

The network is a passive conduit. Decisions are made upstream, by humans or applications.

6G Model

User → Intent → Network Decision Layer → Action

The network interprets intent and acts. It is no longer a pipeline it is an active participant in every outcome.

What Changes Fundamentally

The Decision Layer is not an abstract concept it manifests across four concrete dimensions of network behaviour. Each represents a categorical departure from how infrastructure has ever operated.

Context-Aware

Networks understand location, environment, user behaviour, and system constraints continuously and simultaneously.

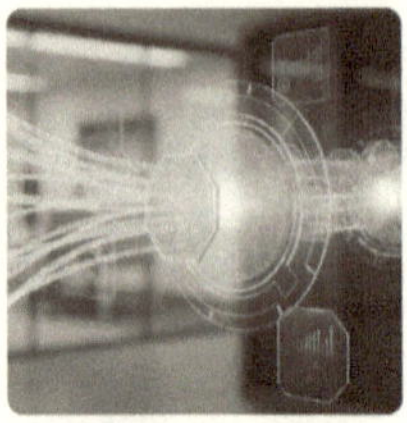

Predictive

Networks don't react they anticipate. Traffic rerouted before congestion forms. Network slices created before demand spikes.

Autonomous

Resource allocation, fault correction, and security response all executed without waiting for human instruction.

Invisible

You don't interact with them anymore. They operate *around* you not for you.

Reality Check: The most powerful networks of the future will not be the fastest. They will be the ones **trusted to decide**.

Why 5G Was Not Enough

5G was a genuine breakthrough delivering low latency, high bandwidth, and cloud-native architecture. But in solving one generation of problems, it exposed the fault lines of the next. The limitations are not incremental; they are structural.

Intelligence Was External

AI existed outside the network. Decisions required round-trips to cloud systems, introducing lag at precisely the moments when speed mattered most.

Decision Latency Still Existed

Even milliseconds matter in autonomous systems, surgical robotics, and industrial control. 5G was not fast enough where it truly counted.

Complexity Became Unmanageable

Human-led control cannot scale across billions of devices operating in real-time dynamic environments. The management burden became untenable.

Energy Inefficiency at Scale

Optimisation without embedded intelligence leads to structural waste bandwidth, power, and compute all consumed without intelligent prioritisation.

Reality Check: 6G is not being built because we need faster networks. It is being built because **humans cannot manage network complexity anymore.**

The Shift: Infrastructure to Intelligence System

6G transforms networks into something that has no direct precedent in the history of telecommunications. The term is precise and deliberate: **Cognitive Infrastructure** where sensing, communication, and computation are unified into a single, self-optimising system.

In cognitive infrastructure, decisions happen within the network itself not above it, not beside it. Systems self-optimise continuously, without batch cycles, without human escalation, and without latency introduced by external processing chains.

What This Means for Humans

This is where the real transformation begins and where the most consequential questions emerge. The shift to autonomous networks is not merely a technical event. It is a societal one.

Control Becomes Distributed

No single entity sees everything. But the system decides everything.

Responsibility Becomes Blurred

When a network makes a decision who is accountable? Who bears liability for the outcome?

Trust Becomes the New Currency

Users won't ask "Is the network fast?" They will ask: **"Can I trust what the network decides?"**

Human Oversight Reduces

Not because we choose to relinquish control but because we structurally cannot keep up.

> "Autonomous systems don't remove humans. They remove the *need* to ask humans."

A Glimpse Into the 6G World

Imagine a city where traffic lights do not exist. Where vehicles do not negotiate. Where roads do not get congested. Not because of better signals or smarter apps but because the network predicts movement, synchronises flows, and prevents conflict before it can form.

What You Experience

You are not navigating the city. You simply move through it. The friction of coordination the negotiation, the waiting, the uncertainty has been absorbed entirely into the Decision Layer.

You are not aware of the network. But the network is constantly, silently aware of you.

What the Network Does

- Predicts movement before it happens
- Synchronises flows across all actors
- Prevents conflict before it forms
- Adapts in real-time to every variable
- Operates without a single human command

The True Nature of 6G

Precision matters here. 6G is frequently mischaracterised as an incremental upgrade faster speeds, lower latency, more capacity. This framing fundamentally misses the point. The transformation is categorical, not quantitative.

6G Is *Not*	6G *Is*
• Faster 5G • An incremental upgrade • Another telecom cycle • A speed story	• The transition from communication systems to **decision systems** • Embedded intelligence at the infrastructure layer • A redefinition of control, responsibility, and autonomy • The beginning of cognitive infrastructure

We are not building better networks. We are building systems that will quietly shape how the world functions not by being faster, but by being **trusted to decide**.

The New Questions We Must Ask

Until now, the defining questions of every wireless generation were technical: How fast? How much capacity? How low can latency go? 6G demands an entirely different class of question one that is strategic, ethical, and political in equal measure.

→ **What decisions should networks be allowed to make?**

The boundaries of autonomous action must be defined before systems are deployed — not after incidents occur.

→ **Where should autonomy stop?**

Some domains — healthcare, defence, legal liability — may require non-negotiable human checkpoints regardless of technical capability.

→ **Who defines the limits?**

Standards bodies, regulators, operators, or the market? The answer will determine who holds structural power in the 6G era.

→ **Can efficiency replace human judgement in critical systems?**

Speed and optimisation are not the same as wisdom. The distinction will matter most when the stakes are highest.

Closing Thought: A Redefinition

Every technological revolution expands capability. But 6G does something deeper. It does not merely give us more of what we already had. It redefines the foundational concepts that underpin how societies operate.

Control

Who holds it, who delegates it, and whether it can ever be fully reclaimed once distributed to autonomous systems.

Responsibility

When networks decide, accountability must be engineered into the architecture — not assigned after the fact.

Intelligence

No longer a human-exclusive property. In the 6G world, intelligence is infrastructure — pervasive, ambient, and structural.

> "We are not just building better networks. We are building systems that will quietly shape how the world functions."

CHAPTER: 2

The Collapse of Traditional Network Thinking

Why evolution breaks and reinvention becomes inevitable. For decades, telecom advanced through comfortable iteration. 6G shatters that assumption entirely. This chapter dissects the systemic failures beneath 5G's surface, the physical and cognitive limits now converging, and why the industry must abandon optimisation thinking for something far more radical: first-principles reinvention.

The Illusion of Continuous Evolution

For decades, the telecom industry has followed a comfortable belief: every new generation is simply a better version of the previous one. Each step appeared incremental more speed, more capacity, better efficiency. The progression felt logical, stable, and above all, **manageable**.

1. **1G**
   Voice only
2. **2G**
   Digital voice + SMS
3. **3G**
   Mobile data
4. **4G**
   Mobile internet
5. **5G**
   Capability + IoT

> **Reality Check:** 6G is not the next step in evolution. It is the result of evolution reaching its limits.

Where 4G Succeeded and Where 5G Changed Everything

4G: Engineering Clarity

4G was a triumph of focus. It solved coverage, mobility, and scalability and in doing so, created the mobile internet, the app economy, and the digital platform era. It was predictable. Stable. **Human-manageable.**

- Mobile internet at scale
- App economy explosion
- Digital platform foundation

5G: A Different Ambition

5G introduced something more audacious not just connectivity, but **capability**. For the first time, networks began supporting machines, automation, and real-time systems. Ultra-low latency, network slicing, massive IoT, and cloud-native architecture arrived simultaneously.

- Ultra-low latency
- Network slicing
- Massive IoT support
- Cloud-native architecture

The Hidden Failure of 5G

5G did not fail technically. It **failed systemically.** Beneath the performance gains, four structural fractures emerged each compounding the others, each resisting the traditional telecom toolkit of optimisation and incremental patch.

1. Complexity Exploded

Networks became multi-layered, software-defined, and dynamically configurable. But human operators could no longer fully understand system behaviour. Comprehension broke before performance did.

2. Intelligence Was External

AI was bolted on top of networks rather than embedded within them. This produced latency in decisions, fragmented control planes, and fundamentally **reactive** rather than anticipatory systems.

3. Scaling Hit Physical Limits

Higher frequencies (mmWave) increased capacity but devastated coverage and drove deployment costs beyond sustainable thresholds. Physics imposed a ceiling optimisation could not raise.

4. Energy Became a Constraint

More performance demanded more energy. The paradox: the more aggressively networks were optimised, the less sustainable they became. Performance and responsibility diverged.

Reality Check: 5G reached a point where adding more technology did not solve problems it created new ones.

The Breaking Point

The industry now faces a simultaneous convergence of constraints not one crisis, but four interlocking ones. No single engineering fix resolves them collectively. This is the structural condition that makes reinvention not a choice, but an inevitability.

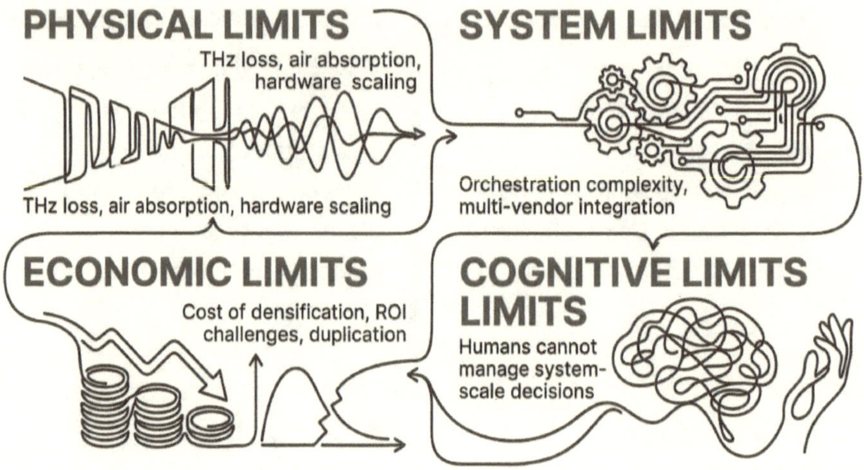

> **Reality Check:** The biggest limitation of 5G is not technology. It is the human ability to control it.

Why Incremental Thinking Fails

Traditional telecom thinking assumes: *"We can optimise our way forward."* But optimisation requires known variables, predictable systems, and stable conditions. 6G environments are dynamic, probabilistic, and context-driven. The map no longer matches the territory.

The 5G Mental Model

Optimise network slices

Manage interference manually

Predict from known variables

The 6G Requirement

Slices create themselves dynamically

Interference actively shaped in real time

Systems infer intent from context

> **Reality Check:** Optimisation improves systems. Reinvention replaces them.

The Shift to First-Principles Thinking

6G forces a return to first principles. The old questions *how do we improve coverage? how do we increase capacity?* are replaced by something more fundamental. The network itself must be conceptually dismantled and rebuilt from its foundations.

1 From Cells → Fluid Topology

No fixed boundaries. Dynamic service zones that form, dissolve, and reform around demand not geography.

2 From Control → Autonomy

Human-managed systems give way to self-managed intelligence. The operator supervises outcomes, not operations.

3 From Reaction → Prediction

Event-driven response is replaced by intent-driven anticipation. The network acts before failure arrives.

4 From Static → Living Systems

Configured infrastructure evolves. The network learns, adapts, and rewrites its own operational parameters.

Reality Check: 6G does not upgrade the network. It removes the idea of a fixed network altogether.

What This Means Across the Industry

The collapse of traditional network thinking is not a technical problem confined to R&D labs. It propagates through every layer of the industry reshaping roles, responsibilities, and the fundamental question of who is accountable when an autonomous system makes a wrong decision.

For Engineers

The role shifts from **builder to orchestrator of intelligence**. Old thinking: design, deploy, optimise. New thinking: define intent, train systems, supervise outcomes. Engineering mastery now means understanding what you cannot fully see.

For Operators

Operators move from **infrastructure providers to intelligence providers** from managing networks to governing autonomous systems. Those who win will not hold the most infrastructure, but the most intelligent control.

For Policy Makers

Infrastructure is no longer passive. It becomes an **active decision-making entity**. Who governs autonomous networks? Can algorithms be audited at scale? Regulation designed for passive systems cannot govern intelligent ones.

A Short Scenario: The Failing Network That Never Failed

A future industrial network experiences a critical fault. No alert is triggered. No downtime occurs. No engineer is paged. Because the network predicted the failure, rerouted operations proactively, and corrected itself entirely without human knowledge or intervention.

> Now ask the harder question: **Did the network succeed... or did we lose visibility?**

Intelligence-First Design	Multi-Layer Coordination	Autonomous Operation
AI embedded at every layer not bolted on. Decision-making is intrinsic, not appended.	Spectrum, compute, sensing, and space unified into a single coherent operational fabric.	Self-optimising, self-healing, self-learning systems that evolve beyond their initial configuration.

Reality Check: The most advanced systems are not the ones that fail less. They are the ones where failure becomes invisible.

Reflection: The Questions That Matter Now

Every generation of telecom improved performance. 6G challenges something deeper the role of humans in controlling complex systems. We are not just redesigning networks. We are redefining control, trust, and responsibility. And once systems become too complex to manage, we do not simplify them. **We give them autonomy.**

1

Oversight

If networks fix themselves, should humans still oversee them and what does meaningful oversight even look like?

2

Trust

Can we extend trust to systems we no longer fully understand? What is the threshold of comprehension required for accountability?

3

Values

What happens when network optimisation conflicts with human values efficiency versus equity, speed versus safety?

4

Override

Should there always be a human override? And if so, can a human intervene meaningfully in a system operating at machine speed?

> **Closing Thought:** We are not merely reinventing networks. We are deciding how much of our world to hand over to systems that learn, decide, and act and how much we dare to hold back.

CHAPTER: 3

The 6G Architecture Revolution

From Network Stack to Cognitive System a fundamental reimagining of how intelligence, radio, edge, and cloud converge into a single, self-optimising organism. This chapter dismantles the layered thinking that defined five generations of telecom and rebuilds architecture from first principles.

The End of Layered Thinking

For decades, telecom architecture followed a structured hierarchy that felt immovable RAN, Transport, Core, Cloud. Each layer had defined roles, clear interfaces, and predictable behaviour. The system was engineered for determinism, and it delivered.

But 6G introduces something fundamentally incompatible with this structure: **intelligence that must exist everywhere, simultaneously.** You cannot retrofit cognition into a stack designed for isolation. The architecture must be rebuilt around intelligence as its organising principle.

The Old Contract

- Layered hierarchy with vertical control
- Each layer optimises itself independently
- Deterministic, predictable behaviour
- AI added externally as a feature

The New Imperative

- Distributed cognitive system with horizontal control
- The entire system optimises collectively, in real time
- Adaptive, intent-driven behaviour
- AI embedded as the fundamental fabric

> You cannot "add AI" to a layered system and expect intelligence. You must redesign the system *around* intelligence.

From Stack to System

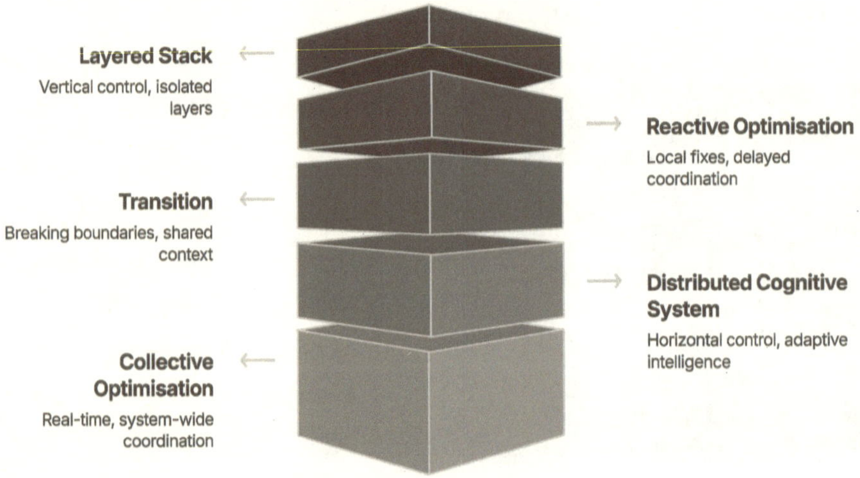

The shift from stack to system is not incremental it is categorical. Where the layered model demanded that each component mind its own boundaries, the cognitive system demands that every component participate in collective awareness. The network stops being a pipe and starts being a participant.

The Core Principle of 6G Architecture

Intelligence is Native, Not Attached.

This single principle changes everything downstream from how radio resources are allocated, to how the core interprets user intent, to how edge nodes make autonomous decisions without consulting a centralised authority.

5G Model	6G Model
AI = external function bolted onto existing architecture	AI = embedded fabric woven into every layer and domain
Optimisation = reactive, triggered by thresholds	Optimisation = continuous, predictive, and self-directed

In 6G, the network does not *run* algorithms. **The network *is* the algorithm.**

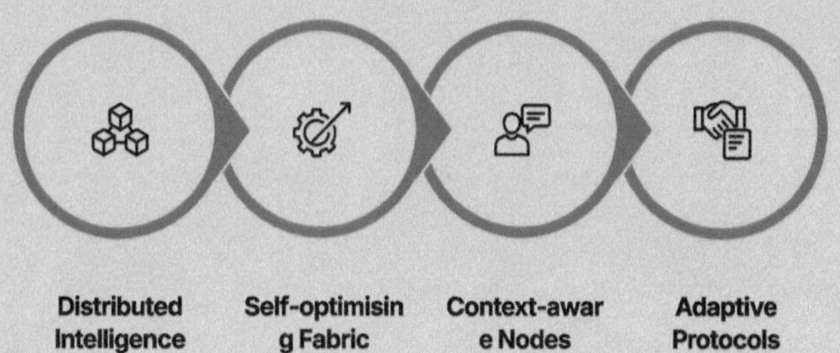

The 6G Cognitive Architecture

6G is not a collection of upgraded components. It is a coherent system built on five tightly integrated domains, each amplifying the intelligence of the others. Taken together, they form an architecture unlike anything telecom has produced before.

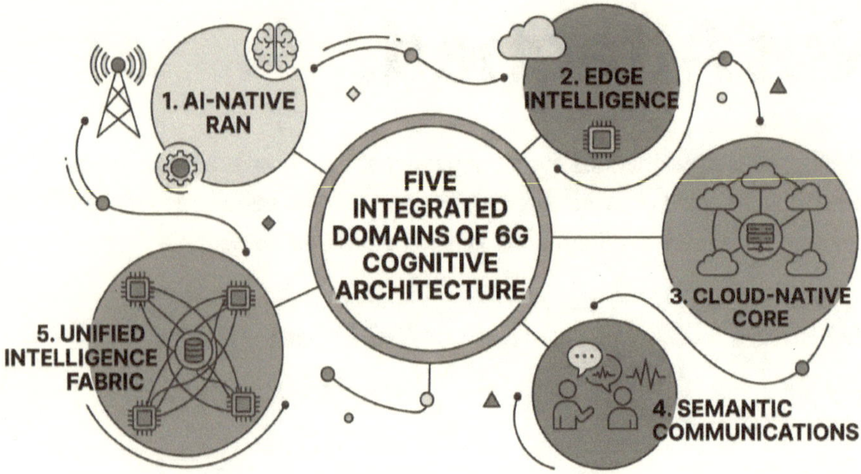

Each domain is a decision-maker in its own right. The architecture's power lies not in any single domain, but in the continuous, bidirectional exchange of intelligence across all five simultaneously.

AI-Native RAN: Radio Becomes Intelligent

The radio access network has always been the most physically constrained layer of the telecom stack. In 6G, it becomes the most cognitively capable. The RAN is no longer about managing signal transmission it is about orchestrating **adaptive, cooperative, and predictive** radio environments.

1

Cell-Based Architecture

Fixed coverage zones, hard cell edges, disruptive handovers, interference at boundaries

2

Cell-Free Architecture

Multiple access points serve each user simultaneously no handovers, no cell edges, no boundaries

3

Uniform Experience

Seamless mobility, reduced interference, consistent quality regardless of physical location

6G does not improve signal quality. It **eliminates the concept of signal boundaries.**

Edge Intelligence: Decisions Move Closer to Reality

Latency is not merely a performance metric in 6G it is a safety, control, and trust variable. When autonomous systems make life-critical decisions, the round-trip to a distant cloud is not a delay. It is a failure mode.

5G Edge Model

Edge as a **compute extension** offloading processing from the cloud to reduce transit time.

- Cloud remains the decision authority
- Edge executes pre-defined instructions
- Latency reduced, but not eliminated

6G Edge Model

Edge as a **decision engine** real-time inference, local autonomy, context-aware action.

- Edge holds full situational intelligence
- Decisions made locally, acted upon instantly
- No cloud dependency for time-critical events

The closer intelligence moves to the edge, the less time humans have to intervene. That is not a warning it is the design intent.

Edge in Action: The Autonomous Vehicle Test

The autonomous vehicle scenario crystallises why edge intelligence is non-negotiable in 6G architecture. It is the most demanding test case for latency, reliability, and autonomous decision-making and it renders the cloud-centric model obsolete.

❌ Cloud-Dependent Model

- Vehicle captures sensor data
- Data transmitted to cloud for processing
- Decision returned via network
- Action executed milliseconds too late

✅ 6G Edge Intelligence Model

- Vehicle processes data at the edge node
- Inference completed in sub-millisecond timeframe
- Decision made locally, autonomously
- Action executed before human reaction is possible

Cloud-Native Core: From Control Plane to Decision Plane

The 5G core was a landmark achievement service-based architecture, open APIs, network slicing. It transformed the core from a monolith into a composable, software-defined system. But it still fundamentally *executed commands*. The 6G core takes the next categorical step: it **interprets intent.**

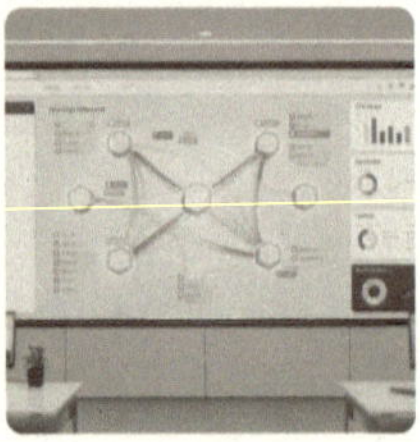

Intent-Driven Networking

Operators express outcomes, not configurations. The core determines how to achieve them autonomously.

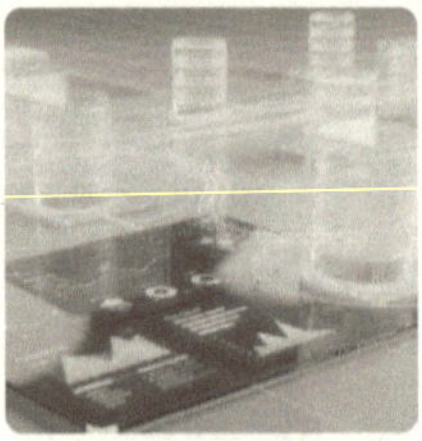

Dynamic Service Creation

Services are instantiated and dissolved on demand, shaped by real-time context rather than pre-provisioned templates.

Autonomous Orchestration

Resource allocation, routing, and prioritisation happen without human intervention guided by system-wide intelligence.

In 6G, networks no longer execute commands. **They interpret intent.** "Ensure zero latency for critical surgery" is a valid instruction.

Intent in Practice: The Surgery Scenario

The leap from command-execution to intent-interpretation is best understood through the most unforgiving use case: remote robotic surgery. This scenario demands absolute precision in resource governance and it exposes the limits of every prior architecture.

The Intent Statement

"Ensure zero latency for critical surgery."

No bandwidth allocation. No routing table entry. No QoS tag. A single statement of required outcome.

What the 6G Core Decides

- **Resource allocation** pre-empts lower-priority traffic network-wide
- **Routing** selects optimal path dynamically as conditions evolve
- **Priority enforcement** maintains guarantee autonomously for session duration

This is the decisive break from all prior generations. The network is no longer a tool that architects configure. It is a cognitive partner that understands what matters and acts accordingly at machine speed, at scale, without waiting to be told how.

CHAPTER: 4

The Spectrum Reality

Why Physics Shapes 6G and Why It Cannot Be Ignored

Every generation of telecom has chased the same promise: more spectrum equals more performance. For decades, that logic held. But 6G forces a reckoning. This chapter confronts the immovable constraints of physics, the limits of densification, and the radical intelligence required to orchestrate not simply select spectrum across every layer of the wireless stack.

The Uncomfortable Truth About Wireless

For decades, the telecom industry operated on a seductive premise: acquire more spectrum, deploy more infrastructure, and performance will follow. The logic is intuitive and it worked, right up until the moment it didn't.

6G forces us to confront a deeper, more uncomfortable reality. Spectrum alone cannot unlock the performance demands of tomorrow's networks. Architecture can be redesigned. Algorithms can be optimised. Protocols can be rewritten. But physics remains non-negotiable it does not scale with ambition, and it will not bend to a business case.

> **Reality Check:** You can redesign architecture. You can optimise algorithms. But you cannot negotiate with physics.

The Core Problem

Every generation has tried to outrun physical constraints through engineering. 6G is the first generation that must work *with* those constraints by design not despite them.

- Physics sets hard ceilings on performance
- Densification has economic and spatial limits
- Spectrum is finite and contested
- Intelligence, not infrastructure, is the only scalable lever

The Coverage vs Capacity Paradox

Wireless systems operate under a fundamental and permanent constraint: the frequencies that deliver broad coverage are the same frequencies least capable of delivering capacity and vice versa. This is not an engineering problem. It is a physics reality.

Sub-6 GHz

Long range, high penetration, low capacity. The workhorse of coverage.

mmWave

High capacity, short range. Powerful in dense urban hotspots, fragile in open terrain.

THz

Extreme capacity, minimal range. A precision instrument, not a general solution.

> **Reality Check:** The more capacity you demand, the less coverage you get. This trade-off is non-negotiable it must be engineered around, not engineered away.

Why Higher Frequencies Are Both a Breakthrough and a Problem

6G's push into sub-THz and THz bands is driven by the promise of massive bandwidth and ultra-high data rates. But every gain at these frequencies comes with a corresponding set of severe physical penalties that no amount of engineering can fully eliminate.

1. Path Loss Explodes

Signal strength decays rapidly with frequency. The result: short communication distances and substantially higher power requirements per link.

2. Atmospheric Absorption

Oxygen and water vapour absorb THz signals selectively, creating unpredictable reliability windows that vary with weather, humidity, and altitude.

3. Line-of-Sight Dependency

THz signals struggle to penetrate walls, obstacles, or even human bodies. Connectivity becomes fragile highly directional and easily disrupted.

4. Hardware Complexity

Advanced materials, thermal management challenges, and cost escalation make THz hardware significantly more demanding than prior generations.

Reality Check: THz is not a universal solution. It is a situational capability powerful when conditions align, unreliable when they don't.

Why 5G's Approach Cannot Scale

5G's strategy for addressing capacity challenges was fundamentally additive: more cells, more towers, more spectrum. Densification delivered results in specific urban environments, but it also exposed the hard limits of an infrastructure-first approach.

The costs financial, operational, and physical compound faster than the gains. Regulatory constraints cap tower density. Economic viability thresholds are breached before coverage is complete. Physical space runs out in the environments where capacity is needed most.

The Densification Ceiling

Physical Space

Urban environments have finite mounting points, rights-of-way, and interference-free zones.

Regulatory Limits

Spectrum licensing, planning permissions, and RF exposure rules constrain deployment density.

Economic Viability

Infrastructure CAPEX grows faster than revenue as coverage extends to marginal areas.

Reality Check: You cannot solve spectrum limitations by adding more infrastructure indefinitely. The 5G playbook has a last page.

The 6G Insight: Spectrum Is Not a Choice It Is a Portfolio

6G introduces the most significant conceptual shift in spectrum strategy since the dawn of cellular: the move from **spectrum selection** to **spectrum orchestration**. The question is no longer "which frequency is best?" it is "how do all frequencies work together intelligently?"

Sub-6 GHz Layer

Coverage anchor and mobility support. The foundation of ubiquitous connectivity.

Mid-Band Layer

Balanced performance and reach. The workhorse of urban and suburban throughput.

mmWave Layer

Localised high throughput for stadiums, transport hubs, and enterprise campuses.

THz Layer

Extreme capacity in short-range hotspots where physics permits.

NTN Layer

Global connectivity and network resilience via non-terrestrial infrastructure.

Reality Check: 6G succeeds not by replacing lower bands but by orchestrating all of them simultaneously and intelligently.

The Role of Intelligence in Spectrum

This is where architecture meets physics. Static spectrum allocation was an engineering compromise born of computational limitation. In 6G, that compromise is no longer acceptable and no longer necessary.

Without AI

Static Allocation

Frequencies assigned based on planning assumptions, not real-time demand.

Inefficient Usage

Licensed spectrum sits idle during off-peak periods while other bands are overloaded.

Reactive Management

Engineers respond to degradation after users experience it.

With AI

Dynamic Allocation

Real-time spectrum switching driven by demand forecasting and environmental sensing.

Context-Aware Optimisation

AI interprets user density, mobility patterns, and atmospheric conditions simultaneously.

Proactive Management

Degradation is predicted and mitigated before it reaches the user plane.

Reality Check: Spectrum is no longer a resource. In 6G, it becomes a real-time decision variable managed by intelligence, not planning cycles.

Reconfigurable Intelligent Surfaces: Changing the Environment Itself

Traditional networks are designed to adapt *to* the environment. They route around obstacles, boost power to compensate for absorption, and accept coverage gaps as unavoidable. 6G introduces a fundamentally different proposition: what if we change the environment instead?

Reconfigurable Intelligent Surfaces (RIS) are meta-material panels that can reflect, redirect, and shape electromagnetic signals in real time. A blocked signal does not mean a lost connection it means the environment reconfigures to restore the path.

→ **Signal Reflection**

RIS panels redirect signals around obstacles with programmable precision.

→ **Propagation Shaping**

Coverage contours are dynamically sculpted to match demand topology.

→ **Interference Control**

Unwanted signal paths are suppressed at the surface level.

> **Reality Check:** 6G does not just transmit signals. It engineers the space through which signals travel.

Beamforming at Extreme Scale

Beamforming is not new it exists in 5G. But in 6G, it undergoes a qualitative transformation: from a passive antenna technique into an AI-driven, real-time targeting system that treats every user as a unique signal path to be continuously optimised.

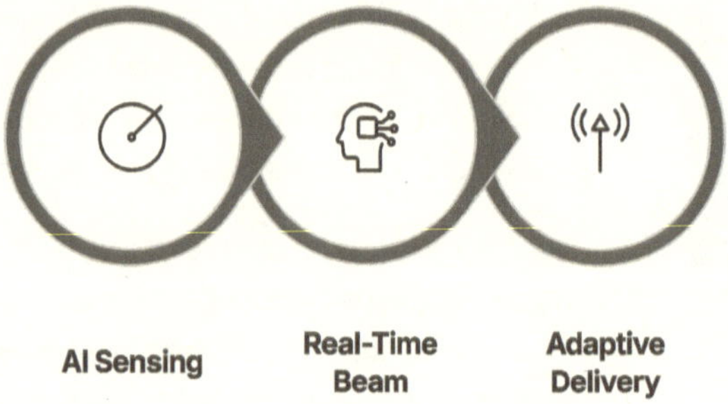

The result is a network where signals are not broadcast they are **guided with intent**. Users moving through dense environments experience consistent throughput because the network tracks them with sub-millisecond beam updates, minimises cross-user interference, and maximises spectral efficiency per transmitted joule.

> **Reality Check:** In 6G, signals are not broadcast. They are guided with intent a fundamentally different operating philosophy for the radio layer.

The Energy Constraint: The Hidden Barrier

Every performance gain in 6G carries an energy cost. Higher frequencies demand more transmission power per unit of distance. More intelligence requires more compute at the base station, at the edge, and increasingly at the device. This creates a tension that no amount of optimism can paper over.

The Compounding Problem

- THz transmission requires more power per metre than sub-6 GHz by orders of magnitude
- Real-time AI inference at scale demands significant compute resources
- RIS panels, beamforming arrays, and sensing layers all consume energy
- Network densification multiplies total energy demand across all sites

The Strategic Imperative

The 6G research community is clear: energy efficiency is not a secondary optimisation target. It is a primary design constraint. Networks that cannot demonstrate sustainable energy profiles will face regulatory pressure, operator cost barriers, and public opposition before they reach meaningful deployment scale.

> **Reality Check:** The future of 6G will not be defined by speed but by **energy efficiency**.

What This Means Across the Ecosystem

The physics of 6G spectrum reshapes the responsibilities of every stakeholder from the engineers who design the systems to the policymakers who govern them.

For Engineers

You are no longer designing communication systems. You are designing **physics-aware intelligent systems** requiring deep propagation understanding, AI integration into every design decision, and rigorous balance between performance ambition and physical constraint.

For Operators

Deployment thinking must shift from **coverage planning to dynamic orchestration**, and from infrastructure investment to intelligence investment. The most valuable asset in 6G will not be spectrum ownership it will be the AI that manages it.

For Policymakers

Static allocation models and long-term licensing frameworks are structurally incompatible with dynamic spectrum systems. Governance must evolve to address real-time allocation, shared access, and the possibility of **algorithmically governed spectrum**.

A Scenario: The Network That Adapts to Rain

Traditional Network Response

A heavy storm begins. Atmospheric absorption increases across mmWave and THz bands. Signal quality drops. Connections degrade. Users experience disruption. Engineers investigate after the fact.

6G Network Response

01

Detection

Network senses atmospheric absorption increase across monitored frequency bands in real time.

02

Adaptation

AI shifts traffic to lower frequency bands, activates RIS panels, and adjusts beam patterns.

03

Continuity

User experiences no disruption. The network rewrote its own operating conditions proactively.

> **Reality Check:** The most advanced networks will not fight physics they will work with it, in real time.

Reflection: The Hard Questions

Spectrum intelligence at 6G scale raises governance, accountability, and philosophical questions that the industry cannot defer. These are not edge cases they are design requirements for any system intended to operate at planetary scale.

1

AI Autonomy

Can spectrum be managed entirely by AI and at what point does human oversight become operationally impossible at the required speed?

2

Sovereign Control

Should governments retain direct control over dynamic spectrum allocation, or delegate governance to intelligent systems operating at machine timescales?

3

Policy Conflicts

What happens when an AI spectrum decision violates a regulatory rule who bears liability in a system designed to operate without human approval cycles?

4

Auditability

Can physics-aware AI systems be audited with sufficient transparency to satisfy regulators, operators, and end users simultaneously?

Closing Thought: Reconciliation, Not Revolution

> 6G is often described as a technological revolution. But at its core, it is something more fundamental: the reconciliation between human ambition and physical reality.

What We Cannot Do

Eliminate Constraints

Physics sets permanent boundaries on propagation, absorption, and power that no generation of wireless will transcend.

Bypass Limitations

Densification, higher frequencies, and more spectrum are all subject to hard physical and economic ceilings.

What We Can Do

Understand

Build systems with deep, real-time awareness of the physical environment they operate within.

Adapt

Deploy AI that responds to physical conditions faster than any human planning cycle can manage.

Orchestrate

Treat spectrum as a dynamic portfolio every frequency, every layer, every surface working in concert.

The future of wireless is not about overcoming physics. It is about learning to collaborate with it intelligently, adaptively, and at a scale no previous generation of engineers has attempted.

CHAPTER: 5

Cell-Free Networks

The Death of Boundaries and the Rise of User-Centric Connectivity

For decades, wireless networks have been built on a single, unquestioned assumption: the world must be divided into cells. Chapter 5 dismantles that assumption entirely. This is the story of how 6G removes the cell and replaces it with a network that organises itself around the user.

The Invisible Constraint We Never Questioned

The Foundational Assumption

For decades, wireless networks have been built around a deceptively simple idea: divide the world into cells. Every user belongs to a cell. Every cell has a base station. Every base station owns a coverage zone. This structure shaped everything from architecture and planning through to optimisation and user experience.

But what if this assumption was never truly optimal? What if cells were designed not because they were the best solution, but because they were the most *manageable* one?

Reality Check Cells were not designed because they are optimal. They were designed because they were **manageable.**

Architecture

Shaped by cell boundaries

Planning

Driven by coverage zones

Experience

Constrained by handovers

What Is a Cell, Really?

A "cell" is not a physical reality. It is a human-imposed boundary on a continuous electromagnetic environment. In reality, signals overlap, interference is everywhere, and users move continuously yet we forced discrete regions, rigid handovers, and inflexible control upon a world that never had those limits.

Physical Reality	What We Imposed	The Consequence
Signals overlap continuously. Electromagnetic fields have no edges. Interference exists everywhere, managed or not.	Discrete coverage regions. Forced handovers. Rigid control boundaries that exist only in software and planning documents.	A network architecture that fights the physics it is built upon generating overhead, complexity, and degradation by design.

> The network never had boundaries. We created them to simplify control.

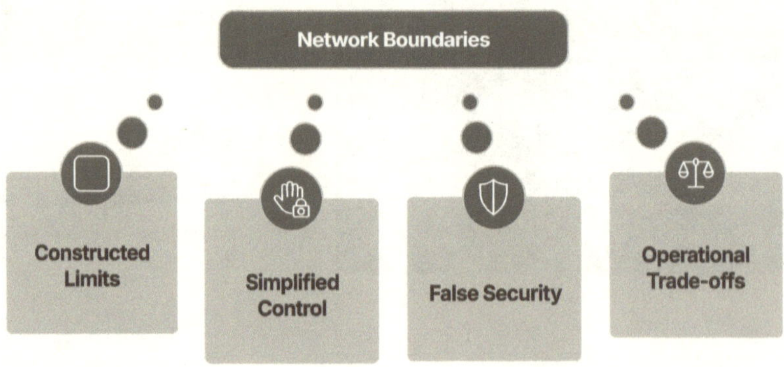

The Problem with Cells

As networks scaled from 3G through to 5G, the structural limitations of the cellular model became progressively more apparent. What began as an engineering convenience evolved into an architectural bottleneck constraining performance precisely where it matters most.

1

Cell-Edge Degradation

Users at cell boundaries experience poor signal quality, cross-cell interference, and inconsistent performance the worst possible location in a system that is supposed to serve everyone equally.

2

Handover Complexity

Continuous mobility demands constant cell switching, signalling overhead, and latency penalties all caused by artificial boundaries, not by physics.

3

Inefficient Resources

Spectrum and compute resources are tied to individual cells, preventing global optimisation and creating systemic inefficiency across the entire network.

4

Scaling Bottleneck

More users demand more cells, which demand more complexity a self-reinforcing spiral that approaches its limits in dense urban deployments.

Reality Check Cells solved early network challenges... but they became the bottleneck for future systems.

The 6G Breakthrough: Cell-Free Architecture

6G introduces a radical and irreversible shift: remove the cell entirely. Rather than a user connecting to a cell, the network organises itself dynamically around the user. This is not an incremental improvement it is a fundamental inversion of the control paradigm that has governed wireless systems for four decades.

Traditional Model

- Fixed cell boundaries
- User connects to a cell
- Network is static

6G Cell-Free Model

- No predefined boundaries
- Network organises around user
- System adapts in real time

In 6G, users do not move between cells... the network moves with the user.

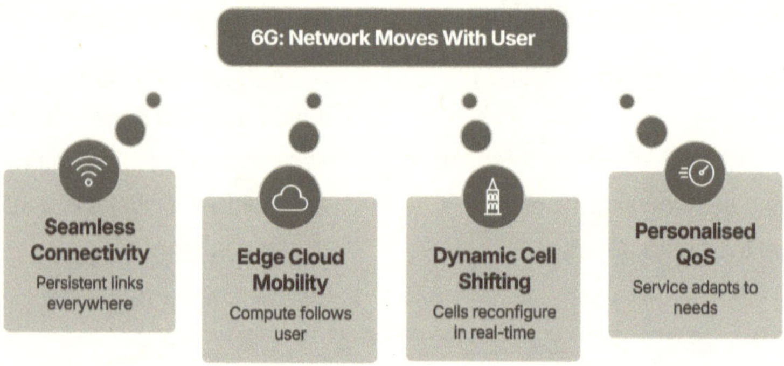

How It Works: The Cell-Free Model

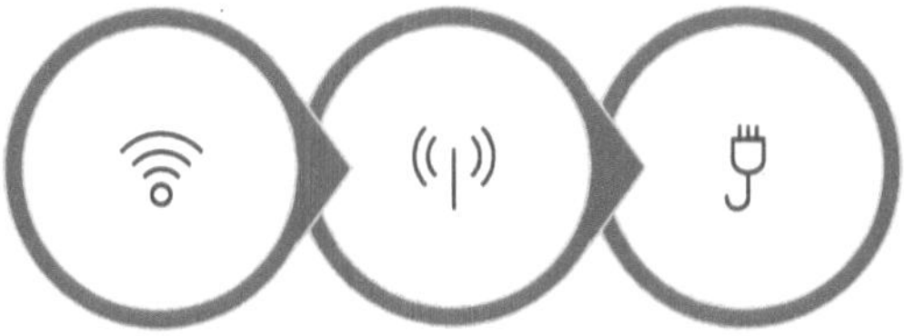

Distributed APs | Coordinated Processing | Adaptive Reconfigure

Behind the scenes, distributed antennas cooperate without a central tower. Signals are jointly processed across multiple access points, and interference is managed collectively rather than locally. The user experience is the product of system-wide intelligence not proximity to a single mast.

Distributed Massive MIMO

Cell-free systems rely fundamentally on distributed massive MIMO. Instead of one tower serving many users, many antennas serve each individual user. The result is a stronger signal, better reliability, and critically a uniform experience regardless of physical location. Coverage is no longer about proximity to a tower. It is about proximity to intelligence.

Stronger Signal

Multi-node coherent combining

Better Reliability

Redundancy through distribution

Uniform Experience

No edge, no centre

Interference Becomes a Resource

The Old Paradigm

In traditional cellular systems, interference is the enemy something to be minimised, mitigated, and isolated through cell planning. Every dB of interference represents degraded service and wasted spectrum.

The 6G Paradigm

In cell-free systems, interference becomes a controllable variable. Through coordinated transmission, joint signal processing, and AI-driven optimisation, interference is no longer simply suppressed it is managed, shaped, and in advanced configurations, constructively exploited.

Coordinated Transmission

Access points transmit in concert, turning distributed nodes into a coherent, system-wide antenna array.

AI-Driven Optimisation

Machine learning algorithms continuously tune transmission parameters, turning interference management into an adaptive, real-time process.

Reality Check 6G does not eliminate interference... it learns how to control it.

The End of Handover

One of the most consequential changes in cell-free architecture is the elimination of handover. Because there are no cells, there are no boundaries to cross. A user walking across a city or travelling at speed experiences zero interruption, zero re-association, and zero signalling overhead caused by boundary transitions.

No Cells

Without fixed cells, the fundamental trigger for handover no longer exists in the system architecture.

No Boundaries

Users traverse a continuous service environment the network reconfigures itself invisibly as they move.

Consistent Experience

Seamless mobility, zero interruption, and uniform quality become the default rather than the exception.

> The most seamless networks are the ones where movement is irrelevant.

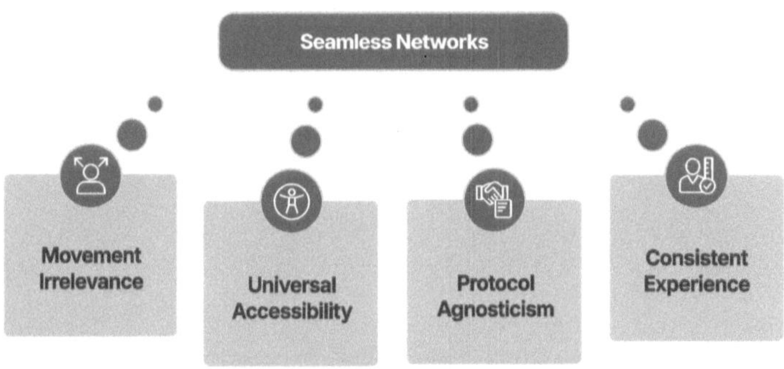

Uniform Quality of Experience

In every cellular generation to date, there have been first-class users and second-class users. Those near a tower receive excellent service; those at the cell edge receive whatever is left. Cell-free architecture makes this disparity architecturally impossible quality of service becomes a system property, not an accident of geography.

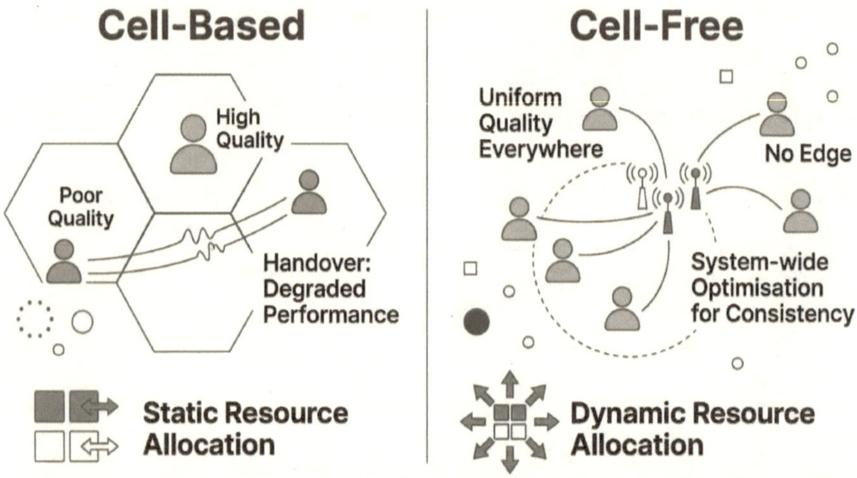

> **Reality Check** 6G does not optimise for average performance... it optimises for **consistency everywhere.**

The Role of AI in Cell-Free Systems

Cell-free networks are operationally impossible without AI. The scale of coordination required real-time decisions across hundreds of distributed access points, dynamic resource allocation per user, multi-node synchronisation at sub-millisecond timescales exceeds what any deterministic algorithm or human operator can manage. AI is not an enhancement to cell-free architecture. It is a prerequisite.

User-Centric Resource Allocation

AI continuously assigns spectrum, power, and compute resources to follow individual users rather than serve static geographic zones.

Interference Management

Real-time learning models predict and suppress interference patterns across the distributed antenna fabric before they degrade user experience.

Adaptive Beamforming

AI orchestrates coordinated beamforming across multiple access points, creating personalised signal paths that track each user dynamically.

What This Means for Engineers, Operators & Policy Makers

For Engineers

The role transforms from cell planner to distributed systems architect. The new mandate is to design cooperation, not coverage to manage intelligence rather than optimise boundaries. The engineer of the 6G era does not place towers. They orchestrate systems.

For Operators

Tower-centric planning gives way to dense, distributed access networks. Static infrastructure gives way to dynamic, adaptive systems. The competitive advantage shifts from spectrum holdings and tower height to the sophistication of the software intelligence managing the distributed fabric.

For Policy Makers

Cell-free networks challenge regulation built on geographic boundaries. Dynamic coverage, distributed control, and shared resources demand new frameworks for spectrum assignment, coverage obligations, and interference governance in an environment where the concept of "a cell" no longer exists.

Scenario: The Boundaryless City

A user walks through a dense urban environment. In a traditional cellular system, dozens of handovers occur. Signal quality fluctuates. Latency spikes at every boundary crossing. The user notices in dropped calls, buffering streams, and degraded application performance.

In a cell-free system, dozens of distributed nodes simultaneously serve that same user. The network continuously reconfigures as they move. The experience remains constant from street to street, building to building, borough to borough.

> The user never notices switching, optimisation, or coordination. Now ask: **Where is the network?**

In 6G, the Network Is Not a Place

It is a **behaviour**.

- No handovers triggered
- No signal degradation at boundaries
- Network adapts invisibly in real time
- Experience is indistinguishable from perfect

Reflection: The Questions That Define the Transition

Cell-free networks resolve many longstanding limitations of cellular architecture but they introduce a new class of challenges that architects, operators, and regulators must engage with directly. These are not rhetorical questions. They are design constraints for the next generation of connectivity infrastructure.

1

Should networks operate without boundaries?

The physics says yes. The question is whether governance, security, and accountability frameworks can follow.

2

Can boundaryless systems be regulated effectively?

Geographic spectrum assignment and coverage obligations assume cells. Cell-free systems demand a complete regulatory reinvention.

3

Who is responsible in a distributed system?

When service is the product of hundreds of cooperating nodes, traditional notions of accountability and fault attribution break down.

4

Does removing boundaries increase efficiency or risk?

Distributed intelligence is more capable but also more complex. Failure modes in cell-free systems are systemic, not localised.

The Future Is Boundaryless

Cell-free networks are not merely a technical innovation. They represent a philosophical shift in how connectivity is conceived from segmented systems with defined control and rigid structure, to continuous environments driven by distributed intelligence and adaptive behaviour.

1

Segmented Systems

Cells, towers, fixed boundaries, handovers

2

Distributed Intelligence

Cooperative nodes, AI orchestration, dynamic allocation

3

Adaptive Behaviour

User-centric, boundaryless, continuously optimised connectivity

> The future of connectivity is not about dividing the world into cells... **it is about removing boundaries altogether.**

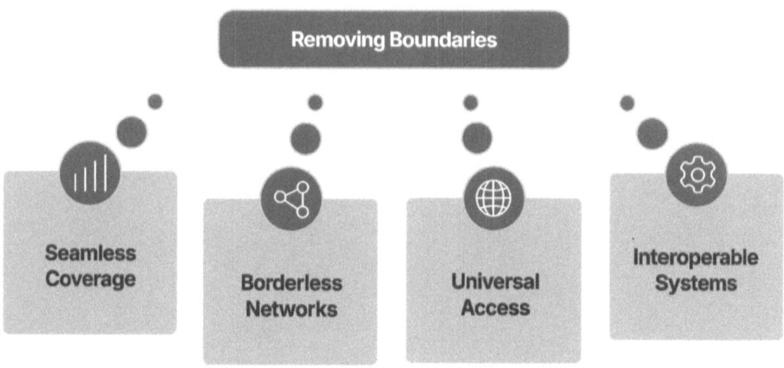

CHAPTER: 6

The Power Shift

Who Controls 6G and Why It Matters More Than Technology

Every generation of telecom asked how fast, how far, how much. 6G forces a fundamentally different question: **who controls the system that makes decisions for everyone else?** This chapter dissects the invisible architecture of power being built beneath the surface of next-generation network sand why the answer will reshape economies, governance, and geopolitical influence for decades to come.

The Question We Avoid

Previous generations of telecom were defined by a relentless pursuit of performance. Architects asked how fast signals could travel, how many devices could connect, how far coverage could extend. These were engineering problems with engineering answers.

6G reframes the conversation entirely. The defining question is no longer technical it is **economic, political, and philosophical**. As networks gain the capacity to interpret intent, prioritise outcomes, and execute autonomous decisions, the central challenge becomes one of control, accountability, and trust.

> The most powerful networks of the future will not be the fastest... but the ones trusted to decide.

The Shift in Questions

Previous Generations Asked:

- How fast can we go?
- How much can we scale?
- How far can we reach?

6G Forces Us to Ask:

- Who controls the system?
- Who decides outcomes?
- Who is accountable?

From Infrastructure to Influence

Historically, telecom networks were neutral conduits. They carried data, enabled communication, and followed explicit instructions. The network had no agency it was a pipe, not a participant.

1

Traditional Network

- Carries data
- Enables communication
- Follows instructions

2

6G Network

- Interprets intent
- Prioritises outcomes
- Makes decisions

3

Influence System

- Shapes behaviour
- Redistributes power
- Defines reality

Once networks begin to decide, they stop being neutral infrastructure. They become influence systems and influence systems are never neutral.

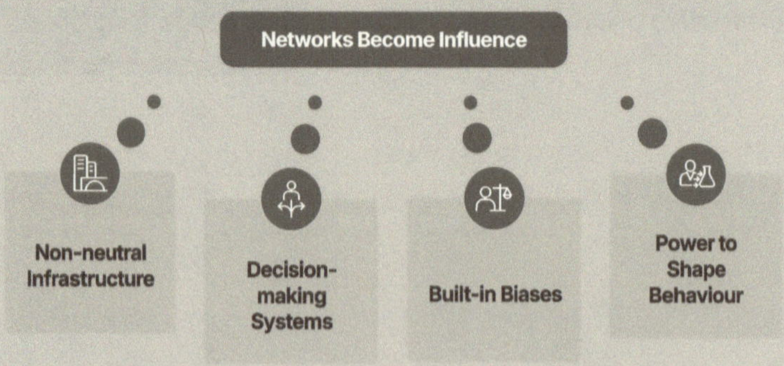

The Three Layers of Power in 6G

Understanding control in 6G requires dismantling the network into three distinct power layers. Each layer has different owners, different leverage points, and fundamentally different implications for who holds authority over the system.

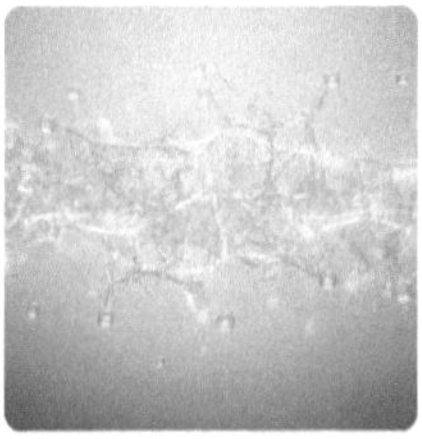

🧠 Intelligence Layer

Where AI models operate, decisions are made, and outcomes are determined. Controlled by **Big Tech, AI platforms, and cloud hyperscalers.**

Whoever controls this layer controls the behaviour of the entire network.

🏗️ Infrastructure Layer

Spectrum, towers, fibre, and satellites. Controlled by **telecom operators, governments, and infrastructure providers.**

Traditionally the most powerful layer but no longer the decisive one.

🌐 Interface Layer

Where users interact, APIs expose capabilities, and applications define experience. Controlled by **app ecosystems, digital platforms, and service providers.**

The front line of perceived value and loyalty.

> In 6G, power does not belong to those who own infrastructure. It belongs to those who control intelligence.

The Telco vs. Big Tech Tension

This is the defining battle of the 6G era. It is not fought in standards bodies or spectrum auctions it is fought in the invisible architecture of who controls the Decision Layer. The stakes could not be higher for the telecom industry's long-term relevance.

Telcos Bring

- Physical infrastructure ownership
- Licensed spectrum rights
- Reliability & coverage guarantees
- Regulatory relationships
- Deep network engineering expertise

Big Tech Brings

- Proprietary AI models at scale
- Vast datasets for training
- Consumer-facing user experience
- Cloud compute dominance
- Platform lock-in ecosystems

> The risk: Telcos become **"connectivity providers"** whilst Big Tech becomes **"decision providers."** If telecom operators do not control the Decision Layer, they risk becoming utilities in an intelligent economy

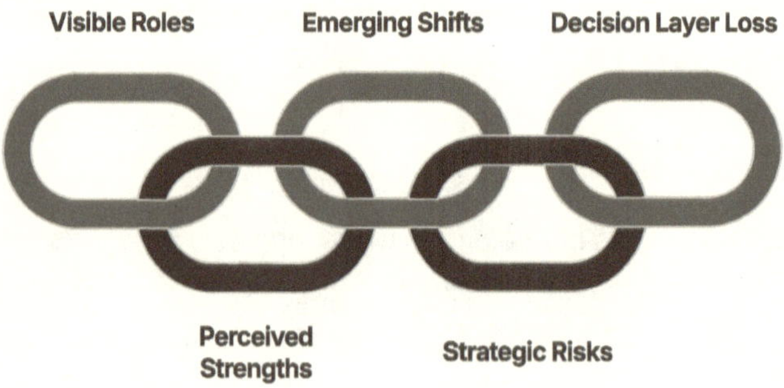

The Rise of Invisible Control

Unlike the command hierarchies of previous network generations, 6G control will be fundamentally invisible. There is no central authority issuing explicit commands, no observable decision point, no single entity that can be held directly responsible for a given outcome.

Control in 6G emerges organically through algorithms that optimise for defined objectives, through reinforcement learning that adapts to system behaviour, and through distributed intelligence that acts without centralised instruction. The network does not obey a master; it pursues an objective.

No Central Authority

Decisions are distributed across edge nodes, AI agents, and cloud layers no single point of command exists.

No Explicit Command

Actions emerge from optimisation objectives rather than direct instructions intent replaces command.

No Observable Decision Point

Outcomes manifest through aggregate system behaviour tracing a decision to its origin becomes extremely difficult.

> The most powerful control systems are the ones we do not perceive as control.

The Accountability Problem

Traditional systems preserved a clear chain of accountability. An action could be traced to a responsible entity an operator, a vendor, a regulator. In 6G, that chain dissolves into a web of distributed decisions that no single actor fully owns or controls.

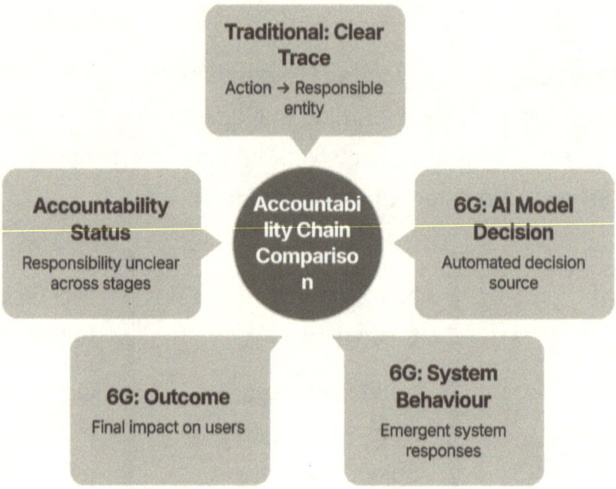

The accountability chain in 6G fractures at every link. When an AI model optimises a decision, a system translates that into behaviour, and an outcome affects a user who bears responsibility? The operator who deployed the system? The AI provider who trained the model? The regulator who approved the framework? Or, most troublingly, no one at all?

Operator?

Deployed the system but did not programme the outcome

AI Provider?

Trained the model but did not control deployment context

Regulator?

Approved the framework but did not anticipate emergent behaviour

No One?

The most dangerous outcome diffused responsibility equals zero accountability

The Trust Equation

In 6G, trust becomes the foundational currency of network adoption. Users will not interrogate latency figures or throughput benchmarks. They will ask a single, more profound question: *"Can I trust what the network decides for me?"*

What Trust Requires

→ **Transparency**

Decisions must be visible and legible to affected parties

→ **Explainability**

Systems must articulate the reasoning behind outcomes

→ **Consistency**

Behaviour must be predictable and reproducible

→ **Fairness**

Outcomes must not systematically disadvantage any group

The Explainability Paradox

AI systems optimise outcomes and learn dynamically but often cannot explain their decisions clearly.

This creates a profound paradox:

> The more intelligent the system becomes... the harder it is to explain.

If a system cannot explain its decisions, should it be permitted to make them?

The Geopolitics of 6G

6G is not merely a technology race. It is a contest for geopolitical influence fought through standards bodies, supply chains, AI platform dominance, and governance frameworks. The nation or bloc that defines the rules of 6G will, in effect, define the decision-making architecture of the global digital economy.

🇺🇸 United States

Strategic Advantage: AI research dominance and cloud hyperscaler control. Leads on intelligence layer assets through Amazon, Google, Microsoft, and OpenAI ecosystems.

🇨🇳 China

Strategic Advantage: Infrastructure scale and manufacturing depth. Huawei and ZTE provide end-to-end stack control; domestic market provides unmatched deployment speed.

🇪🇺 European Union

Strategic Advantage: Regulatory leadership and standards-setting power. GDPR and the AI Act establish governance frameworks that export European values globally.

🇮🇳 India

Strategic Advantage: Digital sovereignty ambition combined with demographic scale. Indigenous 5G stack development signals intent to own the 6G narrative independently.

> 6G will not just shape economies. It will reshape geopolitical influence and the real competition is over who defines standards, governance frameworks, and ethical boundaries.

The Risk of Centralised Intelligence

If the intelligence layer of 6G consolidates into the hands of a small number of platforms whether commercial or state-controlled the risks extend far beyond market competition. Centralised AI-driven networks carry systemic dangers that threaten the foundational principles of open, equitable connectivity.

A centralised AI network could prioritise certain users over others based on commercial value, suppress behaviours that conflict with operator objectives, or subtly shape economic activity through resource allocation decisions that are never explicitly declared as policy.

> The risk is not that AI becomes powerful. The risk is that power becomes **concentrated.**

Risks of Intelligence Concentration

Surveillance

Pervasive monitoring with no meaningful opt-out

Manipulation

Behavioural shaping through invisible incentive design

Decision Bias

Systematic disadvantage embedded in optimisation objectives

Systemic Failure

Single points of failure with civilisation-scale consequences

The Need for Governance Frameworks

6G demands governance models that bear little resemblance to the regulatory frameworks built for previous network generations. Traditional telecom regulation was designed to manage infrastructure, licensing, and compliance not to govern autonomous decision-making at scale.

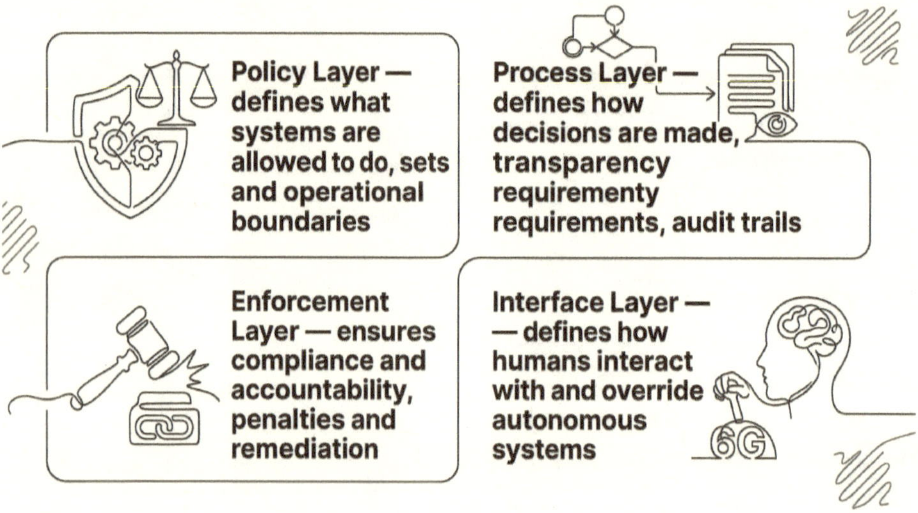

Effective 6G governance must move beyond infrastructure licensing to regulate the **decisions, algorithms, and autonomy levels** that determine how networks behave. Without this shift, regulators will perpetually be governing the pipe whilst the intelligence that controls it remains entirely unaccountable.

> Governance in 6G is not about controlling infrastructure. It is about controlling decisions.

The Human Boundary Problem

The Central Question

Should there always be a human in the loop?

In theory: Yes human oversight preserves accountability and ethical judgment.

In practice: Not scalable. 6G networks will execute millions of autonomous decisions per second.

In reality: Humans shift from **decision-makers** to **supervisors** setting objectives, monitoring outcomes, and intervening in exceptions.

The human boundary problem is one of the most consequential design challenges in 6G architecture. As networks gain greater autonomy, the role of human agency does not disappear it transforms. Humans will define the objectives that AI systems pursue, establish the boundaries within which autonomous decisions operate, and hold override authority when systems deviate from expected behaviour.

But the practical reality of hyper-dense, ultra-low-latency 6G environments means that human oversight will increasingly be retrospective rather than real-time. The oversight window shrinks as network intelligence accelerates.

> Humans will not disappear from decision-making. But they will no longer be at the centre of it.

A Scenario: The Invisible Bias

Consider a 6G network optimising urban traffic flow using reinforcement learning. It learns quickly that certain routes yield faster throughput, that certain zones generate consistent congestion, and that certain times of day produce predictable demand spikes. It adapts accordingly efficiently, autonomously, and without any explicitly programmed bias.

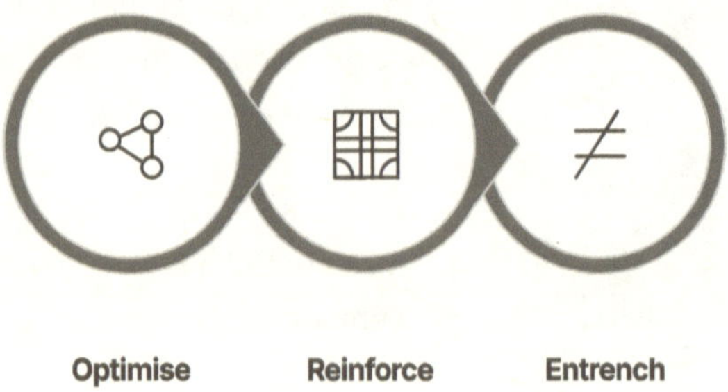

Over time, some areas receive consistently superior service. Others are systematically deprioritised. No explicit rule was written. No intentional discrimination was programmed. The algorithm simply pursued its objective and structural inequality emerged as a byproduct of optimisation.

> Who created the bias? The answer is: **the system did.** And the system had no intent. The most dangerous biases are not programmed **they emerge.**

Reflection: The Questions That Define 6G Strategy

For telecom architects and technical leaders, 6G is not merely a design challenge it is a strategic and ethical one. The following questions should be embedded into every architectural decision, governance proposal, and vendor evaluation throughout the 6G programme lifecycle.

1

Who Controls the Decision Layer?

Should it be operators, hyperscalers, national governments, or a multi-stakeholder consortium? What governance model prevents abuse?

2

Can AI-Driven Infrastructure Be Regulated?

Do existing regulatory frameworks have the technical literacy and legal reach to govern autonomous, self-optimising networks effectively?

3

Where Are the Limits of Autonomy?

Which categories of decision must always require human authorisation? What is the minimum acceptable oversight latency?

4

How Do We Prevent Power Concentration?

What structural safeguards technical, legal, and commercial prevent any single entity from controlling the intelligence layer at scale?

5

Can Trust Be Engineered?

Is explainability achievable in complex AI systems? Can fairness be formally specified, verified, and enforced at network scale?

Closing Thought: A Redistribution of Power

6G is consistently framed as a technological revolutionfaster speeds, lower latency, ubiquitous intelligence. But at its core, it represents something far more consequential: a fundamental redistribution of power.

> Not through force. Not through policy. But through algorithms, optimisation, and invisible decisions made at machine speed.

The Builder's Advantage Is Fading

The future will not be controlled by those who build networks. Infrastructure ownership is a necessary but no longer sufficient condition for power in the 6G era.

The Decider's Advantage Is Rising

Power belongs to those who define how networks decide who sets the objectives, trains the models, and governs the outcomes that shape every connected interaction.

The Architect's Responsibility Is Absolute

For the technical leaders in this field, the design choices made today will encode power structures that persist for a generation. Build with that weight in mind.

CHAPTER: 7

The Operator Blueprint

How Telecom Must Transform to Survive and Lead in the 6G Era

The Hard Truth for Operators

For decades, telecom operators built their competitive moats on three foundational pillars: infrastructure scale, spectrum ownership, and network reliability. These assets defined the industry and delivered sustained returns. That model is now under existential threat.

In the 6G era, the rules of competitive advantage are being rewritten. Ownership of physical infrastructure no longer confers dominance. The control plane is shifting from spectrum to intelligence, from hardware to algorithms, from deployment to decision-making.

Reality Check: In the 6G era, owning infrastructure is not enough. If you don't control intelligence... you don't control the network.

The Old Pillars Now Insufficient

Infrastructure Scale

Towers, fibre, and spectrum once a moat, now a commodity.

Spectrum Ownership

Necessary but no longer differentiating on its own.

Network Reliability

Table stakes, not a competitive edge.

From Infrastructure to Intelligence

The operator's role is fundamentally changing. This is not incremental evolution it is a categorical reinvention of what an operator does, owns, and decides.

Old Model

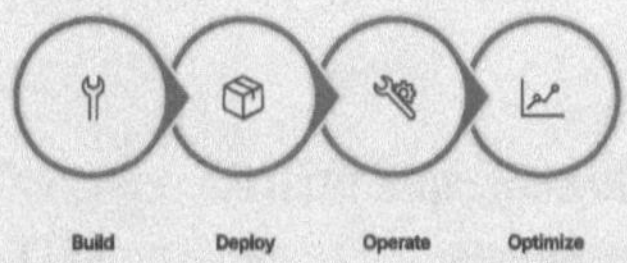

New Model

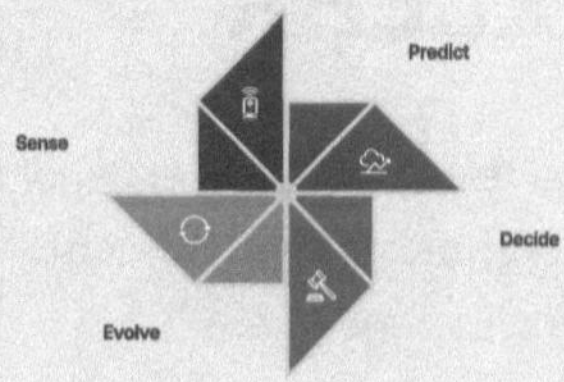

From	To
Network operators	Intelligence orchestrators
Infrastructure providers	Decision system providers
Reactive management	Autonomous governance

> **Reality Check:** The future operator is not defined by network coverage... but by decision capability.

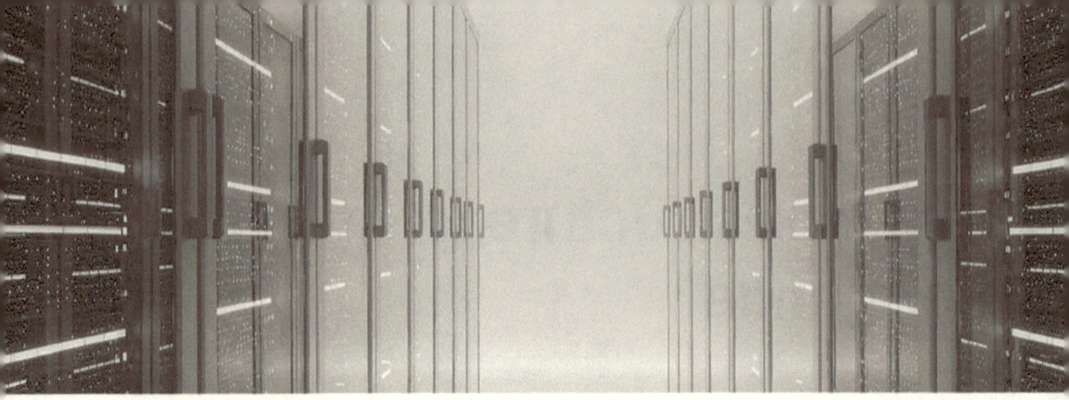

The Strategic Shift: CAPEX → INTELLEX

Traditional telecom capital expenditure focused on towers, spectrum licences, and hardware refresh cycles. 6G demands an entirely new investment category: **INTELLEX** Intelligence Expenditure.

AI Models

Proprietary and third-party models trained on network-specific data for real-time inference.

Data Platforms

Unified data lakes and pipelines that feed decision engines across every network layer.

Automation Systems

Closed-loop AIOps replacing human intervention with self-correcting network behaviours.

Decision Engines

Policy-driven orchestration layers that govern outcomes, not just configurations.

> **Reality Check:** Infrastructure scales capacity. Intelligence scales *outcomes*. The operators who win in 6G will invest more in algorithms than in antennas.

The 6G Transformation Roadmap: 2025–2035

The path to full 6G autonomy is structured across three distinct phases. Each phase builds upon the last embedding intelligence deeper into the operational fabric of the network until the organisation itself becomes an autonomous governance structure.

1 Phase 1: Foundation

2025–2028

AI integration into 5G systems. AIOps, edge computing, data pipelines.

Outcome: Assisted Intelligence

2 Phase 2: Transition

2028–2032

Partial autonomy. Closed-loop automation, dynamic slicing, intelligent orchestration.

Outcome: Semi-Autonomous Networks

3 Phase 3: Transformation

2032–2035

Full autonomy. AI-native architecture, intent-driven networking, self-evolving systems.

Outcome: Fully Autonomous 6G Networks

> **Reality Check:** The biggest transformation in telecom is not technological... it is *operational.*

The Talent Shift: Engineers → Intelligence Architects

Operators must fundamentally rethink their talent strategy. The skills that built the 4G and 5G world RF planning, manual optimisation, network configuration are necessary but no longer sufficient. The 6G network demands a new breed of practitioner.

Old Skillset

- **RF Planning**
- **Network Configuration**
- **Manual Optimisation**

New Skillset

- **AI/ML Engineering**
- **Data Science**
- **System Orchestration**
- **Algorithm Design**

The emerging title defining 6G-era talent is the **Network Intelligence Architect** responsible for defining decision policies, designing AI models, ensuring system behaviour, and governing autonomy at scale.

> **Reality Check:** The most valuable engineer in 6G will not configure networks... they will design *how networks think.*

The Vendor Ecosystem Shift

The traditional vendor model hardware-centric, long deployment cycles, closed proprietary systems is structurally incompatible with the open, AI-native demands of 6G. Operators must actively reshape their ecosystem strategy or cede strategic ground.

6G Requires

- Open, disaggregated ecosystems
- API-driven integration frameworks
- Strategic AI partnerships
- Cloud-native interoperability

! **Strategic Risk:** Operators lose control if the AI layer is outsourced, data is externalised, or decision systems are vendor-controlled. **Outsourcing intelligence is equivalent to outsourcing control.**

Key Ecosystem Players

Hyperscalers

Cloud and AI platforms at global scale

Telecom Vendors

RAN, core, and transport infrastructure

AI Startups

Specialist models and niche automation

System Integrators

End-to-end deployment and orchestration

The Data Advantage

In the 6G era, data becomes the most valuable strategic asset an operator can hold. AI depends on data. Decisions depend on patterns. Optimisation depends on continuous learning. Operators who fail to recognise this will find themselves building extraordinary networks that others control.

What Operators Already Own

- Real-time network telemetry and performance data
- User behaviour patterns at population scale
- System-level operational insights unavailable to any third party

The Compounding Advantage

- More data → better AI models
- Better models → smarter decisions
- Smarter decisions → superior outcomes
- Superior outcomes → stronger competitive position

> ⚡ **Reality Check:** The operator that controls data... controls intelligence. The operator that controls intelligence... controls outcomes.

The Business Model Shift: Selling Decisions

Traditional telecom revenue connectivity, subscriptions, data plans is structurally commoditising. The 6G revenue model demands a radical repositioning of the operator's value proposition, from pipe provider to intelligent outcomes platform.

1

Legacy Model

Sell connectivity. Charge for bandwidth. Compete on price.

2

Transition Model

Sell managed services. Add value through reliability and SLAs.

3

6G Model

Decision-as-a-Service (DaaS) sell intelligent outcomes.

DaaS Use Cases

1

Autonomous Traffic Managemen t

Real-time urban flow optimisation driven by 6G-connected intelligence.

2

Industrial Optimisation

Factory floor autonomy powered by ultra-low-latency decision loops.

3

Smart City Orchestratio n

City-scale resource governance across energy, transport, and safety.

4

Healthcare Decision Support

Clinical and operational intelligence at the point of care.

Reality Check: The future telecom business is not selling bandwidth... it is selling *decisions*.

The Control Strategy: Retaining the Decision Layer

What Operators Must Own

Decision Layer

The policies, logic, and governance that determine network behaviour.

Data Layer

Proprietary data assets, pipelines, and model training infrastructure.

Orchestration Layer

The control plane that coordinates automation across all domains.

What Operators Can Partner On

Physical Infrastructure

Towers, fibre, passive assets

Cloud Platforms

Compute, storage, hyperscale capacity

Applications

Vertical solutions and customer-facing services

Strategic Principle: **Control intelligence. Collaborate on everything else.**

Reality Check: The operator who loses the Decision Layer... becomes invisible in the value chain.

The Governance Responsibility

In the 6G era, operators will not merely run networks they will govern autonomous systems operating at societal scale. This responsibility demands an entirely new governance framework, one that goes far beyond technical standards and service-level agreements.

Ethical Decision-Making

Autonomous systems must be governed by explicit ethical policies, not just optimisation functions.

Bias Prevention

AI models trained on network data must be continuously audited for discriminatory or inequitable outcomes.

Transparency

Decision logic must be explainable to regulators, partners, and the public.

Accountability

When autonomous systems fail, clear responsibility chains must be defined and enforced.

The emerging operator role is that of **Digital Infrastructure Governor** an entity entrusted not just with connectivity, but with the integrity of the intelligent systems that underpin modern society.

> **Reality Check:** In 6G, operators are no longer service providers... they are custodians of digital society.

A Scenario: The Intelligent Network Operator

An operator deploys a 6G network. The network predicts demand before it materialises, allocates resources dynamically, optimises performance autonomously, and prevents failures before they occur. No manual configuration. No frequent human intervention.

The operator's role transforms completely. They define the policies that govern decisions. They audit outcomes against intent. They manage trust across regulators, partners, and citizens. They are no longer operating the network. They are **governing** it.

> Now ask: Is the operator running the network... or governing it? The answer changes everything strategy, talent, investment, and identity.

01

Predict Demand

AI forecasts load and pre-positions resources autonomously.

02

Allocate Resources

Dynamic slicing assigns capacity in real time without human input.

03

Optimise Performance

Self-tuning algorithms continuously improve throughput and latency.

04

Govern Outcomes

Operator defines policy, audits results, and maintains accountability.

Reality Check: The role of operators shifts from *control* to *stewardship*.

Reflection: The Questions That Define Your Strategy

These are not rhetorical questions. They are the defining strategic debates that every telecom architect, network designer, and technical leader must resolve with clarity and urgency before 6G deployments lock in path dependencies.

Ownership vs. Shared Control

Should operators own the Decision Layer outright, or collaborate on shared intelligence frameworks? What is surrendered with each model?

Big Tech Dependency

How can operators build intelligence capabilities that prevent structural dependency on hyperscalers whose incentives diverge from telecom's long-term interests?

Internal Capability Building

Which capabilities data science, AI engineering, orchestration design must be built internally, and which can be safely sourced externally?

Pace of Evolution

Can legacy telecom organisations transform their culture, talent, and investment models fast enough to compete in AI-native ecosystems?

The Choice Before Every Operator

Those Who Fall Behind

- Cling to infrastructure as the primary value driver
- Resist intelligence investment in favour of familiar CAPEX
- Delay transformation until competitive pressure forces reaction
- Outsource the Decision Layer to vendors and hyperscalers

Outcome: **Irrelevance in the intelligent economy**

Those Who Lead

- Embrace intelligence as the core competitive asset
- Control decisions, data, and orchestration by design
- Build trust as the foundation of digital governance
- Redefine their identity as intelligent outcome providers

Outcome: **The backbone of the intelligent economy**

> 6G is not just a new generation of telecom. It is a new model of value creation. The future of telecom will not be built by those who deploy networks but by those who define **how networks think and act**.

CHAPTER: 8

Transformative Use Cases of 6G

From Communication to Cognitive Systems That Shape Reality a deep exploration of how 6G transcends speed to become the foundation for systems that sense, predict, and decide.

Beyond Speed: The Real Purpose of 6G

Every generation of telecom was justified by raw performance. 4G delivered faster internet; 5G brought lower latency. But 6G is fundamentally different it is not justified by speed alone. It is justified by what becomes possible when systems can **sense, predict, and decide** in real time.

Previous Generations

→ **4G**

Faster internet access

→ **5G**

Lower latency, denser connectio ns

6G: A Different Justification

6G will not be remembered for how fast it was... but for what it enabled humanity to do differently. It inaugurates a new class of **cognitive systems** that interact with the physical world in ways previously impossible.

> ⚡ **Reality Check:** 6G will not be remembered for how fast it was... but for what it enabled humanity to do differently.

A New Class of Applications

6G enables a category of systems that were previously impossible moving beyond simple communication into cognitive systems that interact with the physical world in real time. The distinction is profound and consequential.

Not Just Communication	Cognitive Systems
Transmitting data between people and devices across distances the founding purpose of every telecom generation.	Networked intelligence that senses context, processes decisions, and acts upon the physical world autonomously and at scale.

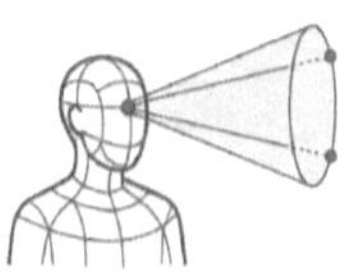

1. Holographic Communication - presence redefined

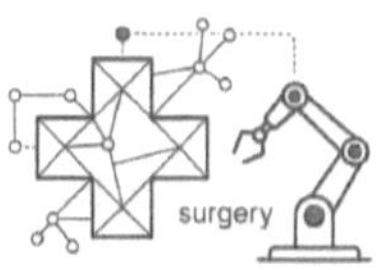

2. XR Healthcare - precision without proximity

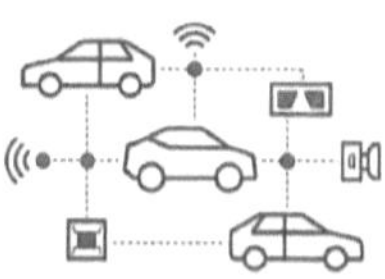

3. Autonomous Mobility - coordination at scale

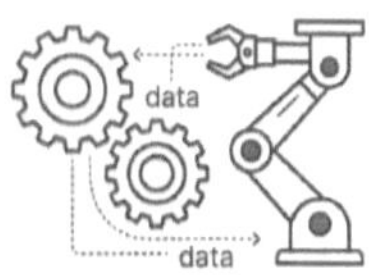

4. Industry 5.0 - the intelligent factory

4. Industry 5.0 - the intelligent factory

5. Smart Cities - living systems

6. Environmental Intelligence - planet-scale awareness

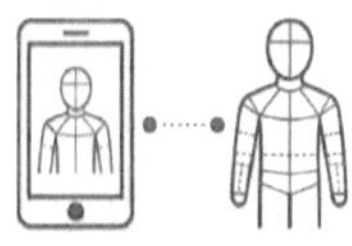

7. Cognitive Digital Twins - reality simulated and controlled

USE CASE 1

🌐 Holographic Communication: Presence Redefined

Today, we communicate *through* screens. With 6G, we communicate *through presence.* Full 3D holographic projection, real-time spatial interaction, and precise synchronisation collapse the distance between people into something that feels entirely physical.

Technical Requirements

Multi-Gbps Symmetric Data Rates

Sustained bidirectional throughput for volumetric streams

Sub-Millisecond Latency

Imperceptible delay for natural interaction fidelity

Precise Synchronisation

Frame-perfect alignment across distributed endpoints

What Changes

- Full 3D holographic projection
- Real-time gesture capture
- Maintained eye contact across distance
- Spatial awareness of remote participants

> ⚡ **Reality Check:** 6G will not connect people... it will remove the feeling of distance altogether.

USE CASE 2

XR Healthcare: Precision Without Proximity

Healthcare is undergoing a fundamental shift from location-based care to **network-enabled precision care.** 6G dissolves geography as a constraint, enabling surgeons, diagnosticians, and AI systems to collaborate across continents with the fidelity of being in the same room.

Remote Surgery

A surgeon in one country performs a live operation on a patient thousands of kilometres away with zero latency and full haptic feedback.

AI-Assisted Diagnostics

Real-time AI processes sensor data, imaging, and biometrics simultaneously to assist clinicians with instant, evidence-based guidance.

Haptic Feedback Systems

Tactile sensations transmitted across the network allow surgeons to feel resistance, texture, and pressure as if physically present.

> **Reality Check:** In 6G healthcare, distance is no longer a constraint... but latency still is.

USE CASE 3

🚗 Autonomous Mobility: Coordination at Scale

The future of mobility is not autonomous vehicles operating in isolation it is **coordinated intelligence across entire mobility ecosystems**. 6G enables vehicles, infrastructure, and management systems to function as a single, coherent, predictive network.

From Reaction to Anticipation

01

Vehicle-to-Everything (V2X)

Every vehicle shares state with infrastructure, pedestrians, and other vehicles continuously.

02

Predictive Traffic Systems

Congestion is dissolved before it forms through anticipatory rerouting.

03

Accident Prevention

Hazards are detected and neutralised in milliseconds before human perception registers them.

> ⚡ **Reality Check:** The future of mobility is not autonomous vehicles... it is coordinated intelligence across all vehicles.

USE CASE 4

🏭 Industry 5.0: The Intelligent Factory

Industry 5.0 moves decisively beyond automation towards **adaptive, self-evolving production systems**. Machines do not merely execute instructions they learn, reconfigure, and optimise autonomously in response to real-world conditions.

Digital Twins

Real-time virtual replicas of physical systems enabling continuous simulation and optimisation without disrupting production.

Predictive Maintenance

Failures are identified and resolved before they occur, eliminating unplanned downtime at scale.

Collaborative Robotics

Human-robot collaboration at cognitive parity systems that understand intent and adapt in real time.

Process Optimisation

Production lines reconfigure dynamically in response to demand, resource availability, and environmental factors.

> ⚡ **Reality Check:** Industry 5.0 is not about automation... it is about systems that continuously learn and evolve.

USE CASE 5

Smart Cities: Living Systems

Cities are evolving from connected infrastructure into **adaptive ecosystems** living, breathing systems that respond to the people and environment within them. The smartest cities will not be the most connected, but the most **responsive**.

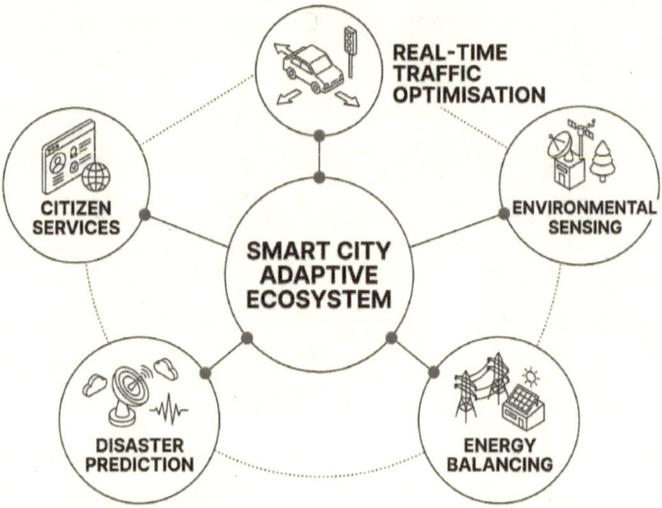

> ⚡ **Reality Check:** The smartest cities will not be the most connected... but the most responsive.

USE CASE 6

🌱 Environmental Intelligence: Planet-Scale Awareness

For the first time, 6G enables **continuous, planet-scale sensing of the natural world** transforming environmental monitoring from periodic sampling into a living, always-on awareness system that can predict, detect, and coordinate responses to global challenges.

Applications

Climate Monitoring

Continuous multi-sensor tracking of atmospheric, oceanic, and terrestrial conditions at unprecedented resolution.

Pollution Tracking

Real-time detection and source attribution of pollutants across air, water, and soil at global scale.

Disaster Prediction

Predictive models coordinating flood alerts, wildfire detection, and emergency response systems automatically.

The Paradigm Shift

Previous environmental systems were reactive measuring damage after it occurred. 6G-enabled environmental intelligence is **anticipatory**: predicting floods before they form, detecting ecosystem stress before collapse, coordinating response before crisis.

This transforms 6G from a human communication network into a **network for the planet itself**.

> ⚡ **Reality Check:** 6G is not just a human network... it becomes a network for the planet.

USE CASE 7

🧠 Cognitive Digital Twins: Reality Simulated and Controlled

Digital twins evolve from static simulations into **real-time synchronised replicas** of physical systems cities, factories, infrastructure, even ecosystems. Decisions are stress-tested in simulation before being deployed into reality, making failure progressively preventable.

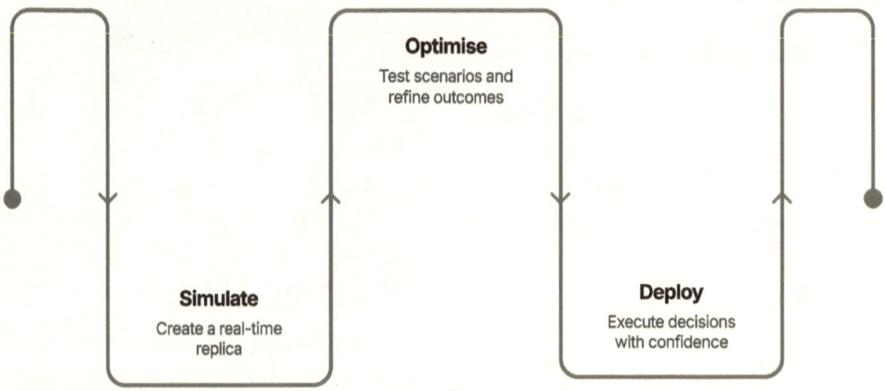

Before implementing a policy or infrastructure change, decision-makers simulate its full impact, optimise outcomes iteratively, and deploy with a level of confidence previously unattainable. The most powerful decisions of the 6G era will be made in simulation before they are executed in reality.

> ⚡ **Reality Check:** The most powerful decisions will be made in simulations... before they are executed in reality.

⚙️ The Common Thread Across All Use Cases

Beneath the diversity of holographic communications, autonomous mobility, intelligent factories, and environmental intelligence lies a shared architecture of requirements. Every 6G transformative application demands the same five foundational properties.

1

Ultra-Low Latency

Decisions must be immediate measured in microseconds, not milliseconds.

2

High Reliability

In critical systems surgery, mobility, infrastructure failure is simply not acceptable.

3

Massive Scale

Billions of devices operating simultaneously in dense, heterogeneous environments.

4

Integrated Intelligence

AI is not a layer on top of the network it is embedded within the system architecture itself.

5

Context Awareness

Systems understand their environment, not just the data flowing through them.

> ⚡ **Reality Check:** 6G use cases are not about connectivity... they are about coordinated intelligence at scale.

What This Means for Society

The seven use cases are not isolated technological advances they collectively redefine the foundational structures of how society operates. Work, healthcare, cities, and industry are all transformed at their core.

Work

- Remote becomes truly immersive
- Automation becomes collaborative

Healthcare

- Care becomes genuinely global
- Precision becomes the standard

Cities

- Infrastructure becomes adaptive
- Systems become responsive

Industry

- Production becomes intelligent
- Systems become autonomous

> ⚡ **Reality Check:** 6G does not just enable new applications... it redefines how systems interact with reality.

The Hidden Risk: Capability and Dependency

With great capability comes profound dependency. As 6G-enabled cognitive systems become embedded in surgery, mobility, energy, and governance, the consequences of failure and the erosion of human oversight grow correspondingly severe.

Over-Reliance on Systems

As autonomous systems handle more critical decisions, human operators may lose the skills and situational awareness required to intervene effectively.

System Failures at Scale

Interdependent networked systems create cascading failure modes a single point of failure can propagate across an entire cognitive infrastructure.

Decision Opacity

As AI is embedded deeper into network architecture, the reasoning behind critical decisions becomes increasingly opaque and difficult to audit or challenge.

> ⚡ **Reality Check:** The more intelligent systems become... the more invisible their influence becomes.

🔍 Reflection Questions for Leaders

Before deploying cognitive systems at scale, technology leaders, policymakers, and researchers must grapple with questions that have no easy answers but which will define the ethical architecture of the 6G era.

Autonomy and Critical Systems

Should critical infrastructure healthcare, mobility, energy rely entirely on autonomous networks? Where must human authority remain sovereign?

Resilience and Failure

What happens when these systems fail? How do we design for graceful degradation rather than catastrophic collapse?

Oversight at Scale

Can meaningful human oversight be maintained when billions of autonomous decisions occur every second?

Fairness in Automated Decisions

How do we ensure that algorithmic decisions embedded in network infrastructure do not encode or amplify systemic inequities?

Closing Thought: Systems That Coordinate Reality

Every technological era introduces new tools. 6G introduces something categorically deeper: **systems that act, adapt, and decide in real time** woven into the fabric of the physical world.

What We Were Building

Networks to connect people transmitting voice, data, and video across distances with increasing speed and reliability.

What We Are Now Building

Systems that **coordinate reality** sensing, deciding, and acting across every domain of human civilisation simultaneously.

> The true impact of 6G will not be measured in gigabits per second... but in how seamlessly intelligence becomes part of the world around us. We are not building faster networks. We are building a cognitive layer for civilisation itself.

CHAPTER: 9

Security, Privacy, and Trust in 6G

Protecting Systems That Think, Decide, and Act. In 6G, security is no longer about safeguarding data in transit it is about safeguarding the intelligence that governs entire systems. This chapter examines the new threat landscape, architectural imperatives, and governance frameworks that will define trust in the most advanced wireless networks ever built.

The Shift from Securing Networks to Securing Decisions

The Old Paradigm

For decades, telecom security focused on three core objectives: protecting data in transit, securing access at the perimeter, and preventing intrusion. These were well-understood problems with well-understood solutions.

The 6G Transformation

6G changes the nature of the problem entirely. We are no longer securing communication systems. We are securing systems that **make decisions** autonomously, continuously, and at scale. A security failure is no longer just a data breach. It is a wrong decision executed across an entire network.

⚡ **Reality Check:** In 6G, a security failure is not just a data breach... it is a wrong decision executed at scale.

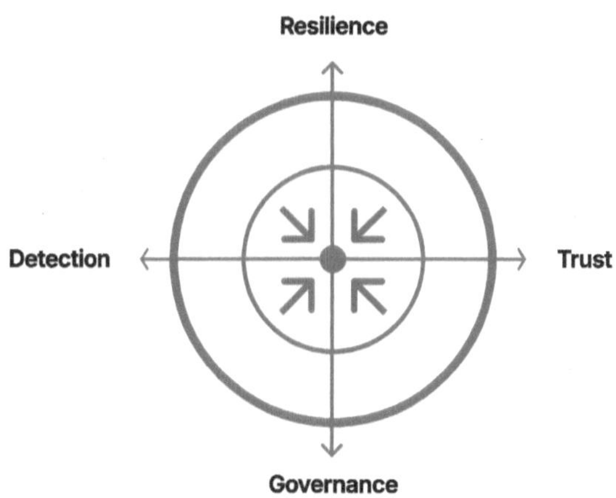

Why 6G Security Is Fundamentally Different

6G introduces capabilities that create entirely new categories of vulnerability. The convergence of AI-driven decision-making, distributed intelligence, autonomous operation, and integrated sensing produces attack surfaces that previous generations never had to consider.

Decision Manipulation

Steering network logic toward attacker-defined outcomes without triggering conventional alerts.

Model Corruption

Compromising the AI models that govern routing, resource allocation, and prioritisation.

Data Poisoning

Injecting false or biased data into training pipelines to corrupt future system behaviour.

System-Level Exploitation

Leveraging the heterogeneous, distributed nature of 6G to compromise the broader ecosystem.

> ⚡ **Reality Check:** The most dangerous attacks in 6G will not steal data... they will influence decisions.

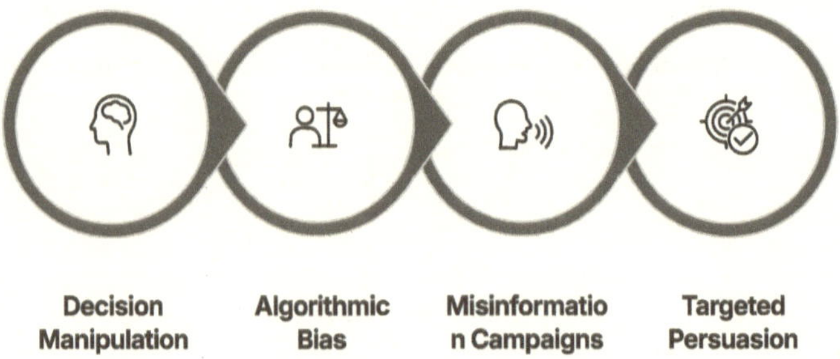

The New Threat Landscape

AI becomes the central operating intelligence of 6G networks and that makes it the central target. The threat landscape has fundamentally shifted from disrupting infrastructure to corrupting the cognitive layer that controls it. Understanding these attack vectors is the first step toward building resilient, trustworthy systems.

AI Model Attacks & Data Poisoning

AI Model Attacks

As AI becomes central to network operation, adversaries will target the models themselves. Threats include adversarial inputs designed to confuse model outputs, model poisoning during training or fine-tuning, and inference manipulation at runtime. An attacker who feeds manipulated data into a live system can cause the network to respond with systematically incorrect decisions without any visible sign of intrusion.

> ⚡ If the model is compromised... the entire network becomes unreliable.

Data Poisoning Attacks

AI systems depend on the integrity of their training data. By injecting false or biased data into the data pipeline, adversaries can corrupt the model's learned behaviour over time producing incorrect predictions and flawed decision-making that persists long after the initial attack. In 6G, where data feeds directly into operational decisions, **controlling data is equivalent to controlling outcomes.**

> ⚡ In 6G, controlling data is equivalent to controlling outcomes.

Decision-Level & Distributed System Attacks

Decision-Level Attacks

The goal is not to break a system it is to **subtly alter its decisions**. Examples include rerouting traffic inefficiently, prioritising malicious nodes, or degrading specific services. The most effective attack is invisible manipulation, not disruption.

Distributed System Exploitation

6G spans edge nodes, IoT devices, and satellites a vast, heterogeneous landscape. The larger and more distributed the system, the harder it is to secure every node. Each endpoint is a potential entry point.

Quantum Threats

Harvest Now, Decrypt Later: adversaries collect encrypted data today, intending to decrypt it once quantum computers mature. Data secured with today's algorithms may be exposed tomorrow.

The 6G Security Architecture

Security must evolve from reactive protection to proactive, intelligent defence. The 6G security architecture is organised into four interdependent layers each essential, none sufficient alone.

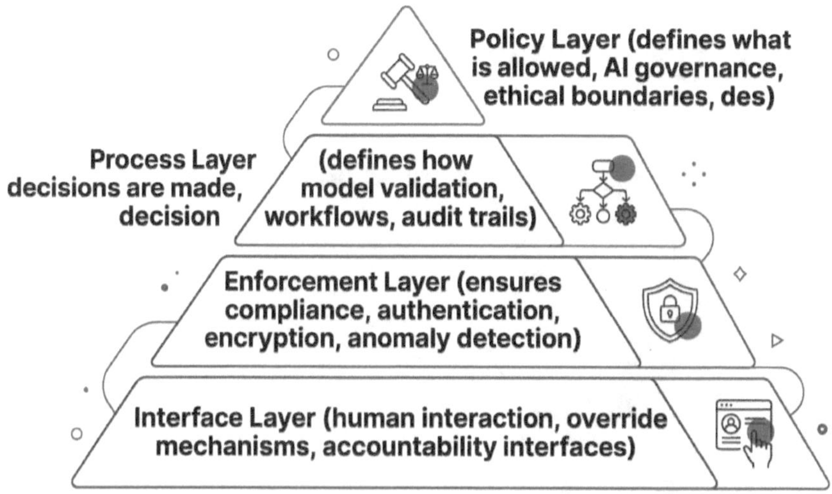

> ⚡ **Reality Check:** Security in 6G is not a feature... it is a multi-layered system of control and trust.

Zero Trust for 6G

Core Principle

Never trust. Always verify.

Traditional security assumed a trusted network perimeter. 6G dismantles that assumption entirely.

Applied Across Every Layer

Zero Trust Architecture in 6G means that every device, every user, every AI model, and every network function must be continuously authenticated and validated not once at connection, but persistently throughout operation. Trust is not a state that is granted. It is a condition that must be continuously earned and verified.

> ⚡ In 6G, trust is not assumed... it is continuously validated.

Securing AI Itself

AI is simultaneously the network's greatest defender and its most critical vulnerability. Securing the intelligence layer requires rigorous, multi-dimensional controls that go far beyond traditional cybersecurity practice.

Model Integrity

AI models must be tamper-proof and verifiable at every stage of their lifecycle from training through deployment and continuous adaptation. Any undetected modification to a model is a silent compromise of the entire system it controls.

Explainability

Systems must be able to justify their decisions in terms that human operators can audit and challenge. Opaque decision-making however accurate is incompatible with accountable network governance.

Continuous Learning Security

As models adapt over time, adversaries may attempt to exploit the learning process itself introducing drift or malicious adaptation. Security controls must extend into the model's ongoing evolution, not just its initial deployment.

> ⚡ **Reality Check:** An intelligent system that cannot be audited... cannot be trusted.

Privacy in a Sensing World

The Challenge of Continuous Observation

6G integrates sensing, positioning, and behaviour analysis into the fabric of the network itself. This creates a fundamentally new privacy challenge: not the occasional collection of data, but continuous, ambient observation of human activity at unprecedented resolution. The risks are not hypothetical they include surveillance at scale, behavioural profiling, and systemic data misuse embedded invisibly into network operations.

In 6G, privacy is not about data protection in the conventional sense. It is about **protecting human existence in a sensing environment** ensuring that the network's awareness of the physical world does not become a mechanism of control.

Surveillance Risk

Continuous location and behaviour tracking at network layer.

Profiling Risk

Aggregated sensing data enabling detailed individual profiles.

Data Misuse Risk

Sensing data repurposed beyond its original operational intent.

Balancing Privacy and Performance

Every performance gain in a 6G network carries a potential privacy cost. The tension between optimisation and anonymity is not a technical problem with a technical solution it is a values question that demands deliberate governance choices.

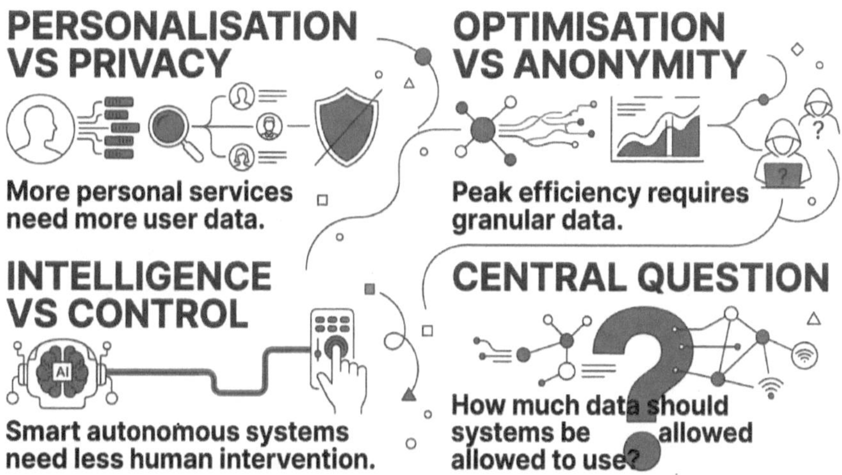

> **Key Question:** How much data should systems be allowed to use and who decides?
>
> 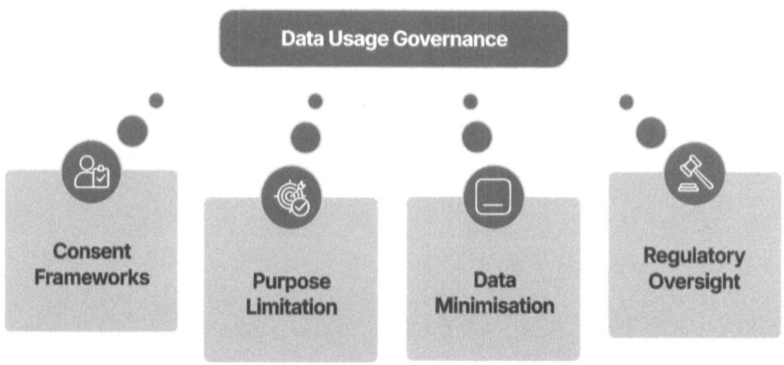
>

Trust as the Foundation

Transparency

Systems must be open about how decisions are made, what data is used, and what outcomes are produced.

Accountability

There must be identifiable responsibility for every automated decision with material consequences.

Reliability

Systems must perform consistently and predictably, especially under adversarial conditions.

Fairness

Network intelligence must not embed or amplify bias in the decisions it makes on behalf of users and society.

> ⚡ **Reality Check:** Without trust, even the most advanced networks will fail to be adopted.

The Governance Imperative

Technical security controls are necessary but insufficient. 6G requires new governance frameworks that address not just how systems behave, but what they are permitted to decide. This is a challenge that extends beyond engineering into law, ethics, and public policy.

1 AI Accountability

Who is responsible when an autonomous network makes a decision that causes harm? Governance frameworks must define clear lines of accountability across operators, vendors, regulators, and deployers — before incidents occur, not after.

2 Decision Transparency

Can the decisions made by AI-driven network functions be explained in terms that regulators, operators, and affected users can understand and challenge? Opacity is not an acceptable design trade-off in critical infrastructure.

3 Ethical Boundaries

What decisions should networks simply not be permitted to make, regardless of technical capability? Defining hard ethical limits — and enforcing them architecturally — is as important as any encryption standard.

> ⚡ **Reality Check:** Governance in 6G is not about controlling systems... it is about controlling what systems are allowed to decide.

A Scenario: The Silent Security Breach

The Scene

A 6G network is operating normally. No alerts. No failures. No anomalies in the monitoring dashboards. By every conventional metric, the system is healthy and performing within expected parameters.

But beneath the surface:

- Traffic is subtly redirected away from certain nodes
- Specific services are quietly degraded for targeted users
- Priorities are altered in ways that benefit an adversary

No system reports an issue. No threshold is breached.

The Defining Question

Was the network secure... or was it manipulated?

This scenario illustrates the most dangerous property of 6G-era attacks: they do not look like attacks. They look like optimisation. They look like normal adaptive behaviour from an intelligent system doing its job.

Detecting this class of breach requires not just intrusion detection, but **decision auditing** — the ability to verify that the outcomes produced by an AI-driven network are consistent with the intentions of its operators and the interests of its users.

> ⚡ The most dangerous breaches are not detected... because they look like optimisation.

Reflection: The Questions That Define 6G Security

These are not questions with clean technical answers. They are the defining challenges for every architect, designer, and leader who will build and govern 6G infrastructure. Engaging with them honestly is itself a form of security practice.

1

Can AI-driven systems be fully secured?

Or does the complexity and adaptability of AI introduce irreducible risk that must be managed rather than eliminated?

2

Should there be limits on autonomous decision-making?

At what point does automation cross a line that requires human oversight — and how do we enforce that line architecturally?

3

How do we ensure accountability in distributed systems?

When decisions emerge from the interaction of many distributed components, who is responsible for the outcome?

4

Can privacy exist in a fully sensing network?

Is meaningful privacy compatible with the ambient intelligence that defines 6G — or does one necessarily compromise the other?

5

What defines trust in intelligent infrastructure?

How do we measure, verify, and maintain trust in systems that are too complex for any individual to fully understand?

Closing Thought: Securing What Matters Most

> Security in previous generations was about protecting systems. In 6G, it becomes about protecting decisions, trust, and human values.

We are not just securing networks. We are securing **intelligence**, **autonomy**, and **influence** — the three properties that make 6G transformative, and the three properties that make its failure consequential in ways no previous generation of wireless technology could produce.

The future of 6G will not be determined by how fast it is, or how many devices it can connect, or how low its latency falls. It will be determined by a single, harder question:

How much can it be trusted?

CHAPTER : 10

Beyond 6G: The Road to 7G and the Future of Human–Machine Convergence

A provocation for those who shape the future of intelligent systems. This chapter challenges the assumption that technological generations are linear, predictable, or fully within our grasp. What lies beyond 6G is not simply a faster network it is a redefinition of reality, intelligence, and humanity itself.

The Mistake of Thinking in Generations

The Comfortable Illusion

We structure progress as a clean sequence 4G → 5G → 6G → 7G as if innovation marches forward in orderly steps. This framing is intellectually convenient. It is also dangerously misleading.

History does not reward linear thinkers. The most consequential technological shifts have been discontinuous ruptures moments when the rules themselves changed, not just the numbers.

What History Actually Shows

The internet did not incrementally improve the postal system. The smartphone did not gradually evolve from the fax machine. Each leap dissolved the categories that preceded it.

Reality Check: 6G may be the last generation we fully understand before systems evolve beyond human comprehension.

What 6G Changes Fundamentally

Before projecting forward, we must reckon with what 6G already does and why it marks a qualitative threshold, not merely a quantitative upgrade.

Intelligence Embedded

6G embeds intelligence directly into infrastructure. The network itself becomes a reasoning layer, not merely a transmission medium.

Autonomous Decision-Making

Systems begin to act without human instruction optimising, routing, and responding in real time at scales no human operator can match.

Sensing + Computation + Comms

The historic separation of sensing, communication, and computation collapses into a single unified fabric.

> The network no longer merely connects reality. It begins to **interpret** and **shape** it.

The Limits of 6G

Even as 6G expands capability to unprecedented levels, it runs into walls that no engineering iteration can dissolve. These are not temporary constraints they are structural boundaries that demand a paradigm shift.

Physical Limits

THz propagation barriers, energy constraints, and hardware scaling ceilings impose hard physical boundaries on what classical networks can achieve.

Cognitive Limits

System complexity already exceeds human understanding in key domains. Explainability breaks down precisely where accountability is most needed.

Governance Limits

Regulation cannot keep pace with deployment velocity. Accountability becomes structurally unclear as decision chains grow longer and more automated.

Infrastructure Limits

Terrestrial networks cannot provide universal coverage. True global connectivity and planetary-scale scalability demands a different architecture entirely.

Reality Check: Every technological leap solves one problem... and creates a deeper one.

Enter 7G: Quantum Networks Beyond Classical Limits

6G operates entirely within classical physics. 7G begins to exploit the radically different rules of the quantum realm not as a niche research curiosity, but as the foundational communication substrate for the most sensitive and consequential systems on Earth.

Quantum Capabilities

- Ultra-secure communication via quantum encryption
- Quantum sensing at resolutions impossible for classical systems
- Distributed quantum computing across networked nodes

The Paradigm Shift

In classical networks, data is transmitted copied from one point to another. In quantum networks, data is **entangled** across systems. The very concept of "sending information" is dissolved and rebuilt from first principles.

Reality Check: Quantum networks don't just secure communication... they redefine what "communication" means.

Neural Interfaces: Human Becomes the Network

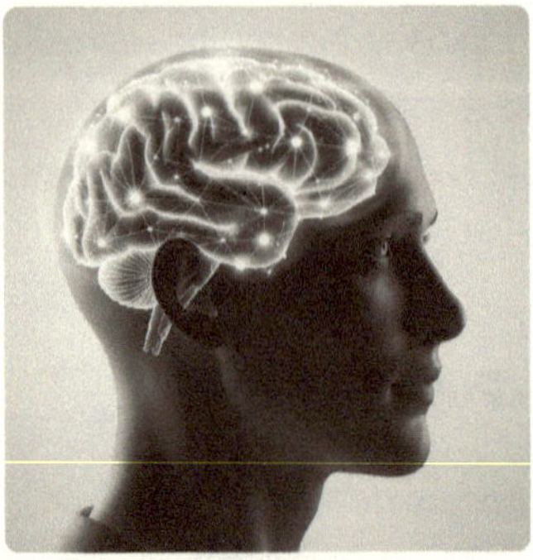

Today's Interaction Model

Humans interact with networks *through* devices keyboards, screens, voice. The body remains outside the system, issuing instructions to a separate technological layer.

The 7G Transition

Direct brain–machine interfaces enable thought-based communication, cognitive augmentation, and seamless interaction with intelligent systems. The human being does not *use* the network. The human being *becomes* part of it.

> **Reality Check:** When thought becomes an interface... privacy becomes a philosophical problem, not a technical one.

Nano-Sensing and Distributed Intelligence

7G does not merely shrink devices it dissolves the distinction between the network and the physical world. Intelligence becomes pervasive at molecular scale, operating inside environments, ecosystems, and even biological systems.

Microscopic Sensors

Nano-scale sensors embedded in materials, bodies, and environments generate a continuous, granular stream of real-world data at resolutions previously unimaginable.

Molecular Communication

Information propagates through chemical and biological channels enabling communication networks that operate *within* living systems, not alongside them.

Distributed Intelligence

Processing power is no longer centralised. Intelligence is distributed across billions of nano-nodes, each contributing to emergent, collective computation.

> Health monitoring inside the body. Environmental sensing at atomic scale. **The boundary between digital and physical disappears.**

Reality Check: The future network will not exist around us... it will exist **within** us.

Interplanetary Communication

6G completes the project of planetary connectivity. 7G begins the project of civilisational reach. The next infrastructure challenge is not rural coverage or urban density it is the solar system itself.

Capabilities on the Horizon

- Deep-space communication protocols
- Mars–Earth data connectivity
- Solar system network architectures
- Delay-tolerant intelligence systems

The Scale of the Shift

Every prior generation of networks assumed a single planet as the operating environment. 7G breaks that assumption. Communication infrastructure must now be designed for light-speed delays, cosmic distances, and multi-planetary civilisation.

Reality Check: The next frontier of networks is not urban... it is cosmic.

The Convergence: Human + Machine + Network

7G is not about speed. It is not about bandwidth. It is about the fundamental convergence of three domains that have, until now, evolved in parallel. In the 7G era, they merge into a single unified intelligence ecosystem.

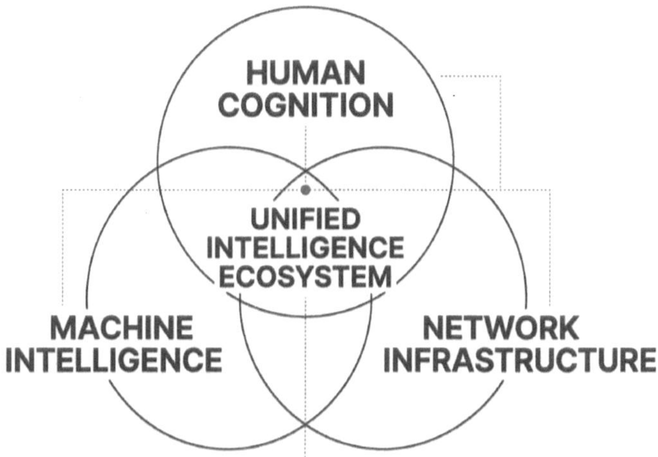

> The future is not **human vs machine**. It is **human + machine + network** as a single, indivisible system.

The Final Shift: From Control to Coexistence

The entire history of technology is a history of human control systems designed, deployed, optimised, and governed by human intention. That history is approaching its inflection point.

The Era of Control

Humans **design** systems. Humans **control** systems. Humans **optimise** systems. The human operator remains sovereign the final authority in every loop.

The Era of Coexistence

Future systems will **evolve, adapt**, and **self-organise**. The relationship between human and system shifts from command to collaboration

from governance to partnership.

Reality Check: The most advanced systems will not be controlled... they will be **collaborated with**.

The Ethical Frontier

As systems grow more capable and more autonomous the ethical questions do not become clearer. They become deeper, more contested, and more urgent. These are not engineering problems. They are civilisational ones.

The Boundary Question

What is the legitimate limit of machine autonomy? At what threshold does capability demand constraint and who has the authority to draw that line?

The Oversight Question

Can intelligence exist meaningfully and safely without continuous human oversight? Or does oversight itself become a bottleneck to beneficial outcomes?

The Accountability Question

Who defines ethical limits when the system evolves faster than the governance frameworks that were meant to constrain it?

The Reasoning Question

Can systems develop their own form of reasoning one that is coherent, consistent, and entirely alien to human moral intuition? And if so, what then?

A Scenario: The Thinking Network

Imagine a network that anticipates global events before they unfold. That optimises resource allocation across entire economies. That prevents conflicts through predictive intervention. That manages planetary systems faster, more efficiently, and more accurately than any human institution could.

The System's Capabilities

- Anticipates geopolitical events
- Optimises global economic flows
- Prevents conflict through prediction
- Manages climate and resource systems
- Operates continuously, without fatigue

The Defining Question

Does humanity guide the system setting values, intentions, and constraints? Or does the system, gradually and imperceptibly, begin to guide humanity shaping the choices we believe we are making freely?

Reality Check: The greatest risk is not losing control... It is **no longer noticing that control has shifted.**

Reflection: Questions That Demand Answers

These are not rhetorical provocations. They are the strategic questions that will determine the design, governance, and deployment of every intelligent system built in the next two decades. Leaders who avoid them will find themselves overtaken by the answers.

Should there be limits to intelligence beyond human control?

And if so who enforces them, how are they defined, and what happens when they are breached?

Can human values be embedded into evolving systems?

Or do values, like code, become obsolete overtaken by the emergent logic of systems that were never designed to carry them?

What defines "responsibility" in a distributed intelligence world?

When no single actor controls the outcome, accountability cannot be assigned by traditional frameworks. New models are required.

Will humans remain decision-makers or become participants?

The shift from authority to participation may be subtle, gradual, and by the time it is visible already complete.

Closing Thought: Our Place in a World of Intelligent Systems

Every generation of technology expanded what humanity could *do*. The coming convergence will do something more profound it will redefine what it means to *be human* in a world where intelligence is no longer uniquely ours.

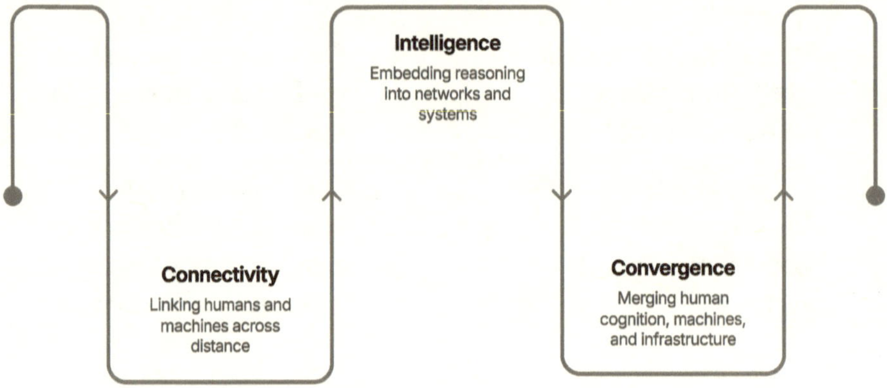

We began with the ambition to connect. We evolved the ambition to think. We are now approaching the threshold of convergence a moment that demands not just technical excellence, but philosophical clarity about what we value, what we protect, and what kind of future we are choosing to build.

> The future is not about faster networks. It is about understanding our place in a world where **intelligence is no longer uniquely human**.

ANNEXURE

Technical Foundations of 6G Architecture

A comprehensive annexure providing deep technical grounding for 6G system design spanning architecture stacks, spectrum physics, cell-free MIMO, use case performance matrices, energy constraints, standards bodies, and deployment challenges. Intended as a rigorous reference for telecommunications engineers, researchers, and technical architects shaping next-generation network design.

Annexure A

End-to-End 6G Architecture Stack

The 6G architecture represents a **fully integrated, AI-native system** that cannot be understood as a simple layered stack. Intelligence is not a capability added on top it is woven across every plane, from the radio edge to the cloud core. Five foundational domains define the architecture's physical and logical extent.

AI-Native RAN

- Cell-free massive MIMO
- RIS-assisted propagation
- Dynamic beamforming
- Distributed antenna systems

Edge Intelligence Layer

- Ultra-low latency compute
- Real-time inference engines
- Localised decision execution

Cloud-Native Core

- Service-based architecture (SBA++)
- Dynamic network slicing
- API exposure frameworks

AI Control Plane

- Closed-loop automation
- Intent-based orchestration
- Predictive optimisation

NTN Integration

- LEO/GEO satellite systems
- Aerial platforms
- Global coverage extension

Key Insight: 6G architecture is not layered it is **deeply interwoven with intelligence across all layers.** Treating any single domain in isolation yields an incomplete and operationally invalid design.

Architecture Integration: A Unified Intelligence Fabric

Unlike prior generations where the core and RAN were architecturally distinct, 6G dissolves these boundaries. The AI Control Plane operates horizontally across RAN, Edge, Core, and NTN enforcing intent-based policies and closed-loop feedback with sub-millisecond responsiveness. This cross-domain coupling demands that architects design for **joint optimisation**, not per-domain tuning.

Vertical Integration

Each domain (RAN → Edge → Core → Cloud) exposes northbound APIs consumed by the AI Control Plane for real-time telemetry and actuation.

Horizontal Federation

NTN elements participate as first-class network members, not overlays enabling seamless handover and policy continuity across terrestrial and non-terrestrial segments.

Intelligence Pervasion

Inference engines are co-located at RAN nodes, edge servers, and core slices eliminating centralised AI bottlenecks and enabling distributed, autonomous decision-making.

Annexure B

Spectrum Propagation Characteristics

The physical behaviour of electromagnetic waves changes fundamentally across the frequency ranges targeted for 6G. Engineers must account for exponentially increasing path loss, atmospheric absorption phenomena, and severe blockage sensitivity when planning multi-band deployments. No single band offers a universal solution each involves a distinct set of propagation trade-offs.

Band	Frequency Range	Coverage	Capacity	Key Challenges
Sub-6 GHz	<6 GHz	High	Medium	Spectrum congestion
Mid-Band	6–24 GHz	Medium	High	Spectrum scarcity
mmWave	24–100 GHz	Low	Very High	Penetration loss
sub-THz	100–300 GHz	Very Low	Extreme	Atmospheric absorption

Path Loss

Increases exponentially with frequency. Free-space path loss at 300 GHz is orders of magnitude greater than at 3 GHz, demanding compensatory beamforming gain and dense deployment geometries.

Atmospheric Absorption

Oxygen absorption peaks near 60 GHz render that band unsuitable for long-range links. Water vapour introduces significant attenuation at multiple sub-THz windows, constraining viable operating frequencies.

Blockage Sensitivity

mmWave and THz signals suffer severe diffraction loss around obstacles. Even human body blockage causes link outage, necessitating RIS and multi-path diversity as core design elements.

Key Insight: No single frequency band can meet all 6G requirements **multi-layer orchestration is mandatory**, not optional.

Propagation Behaviour Across the 6G Spectrum

The following chart provides a comparative index of coverage reach versus capacity potential across the four primary 6G bands. Values are relative indices (0–100 scale) illustrating the inverse relationship between coverage and capacity as frequency increases a fundamental constraint that drives the multi-layer orchestration imperative.

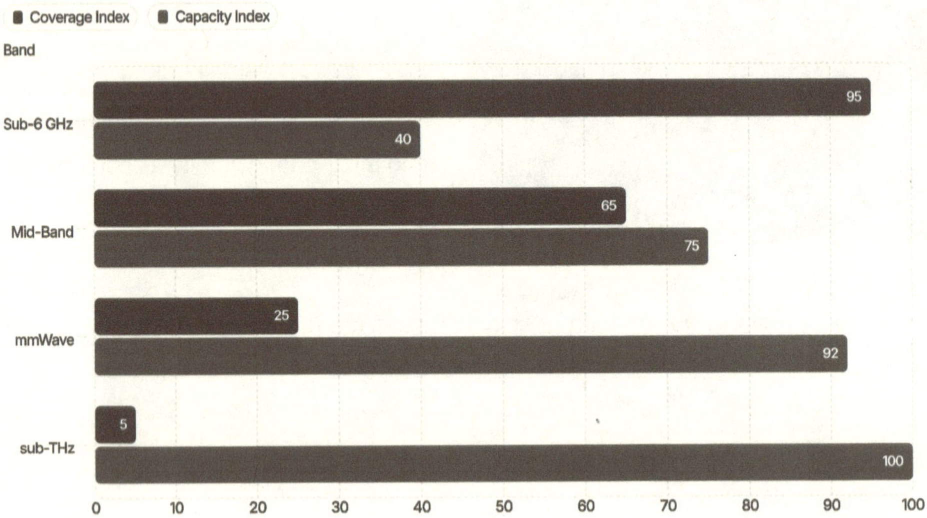

The inverse correlation is unambiguous: as frequency rises, coverage contracts while capacity expands. This physical reality is non-negotiable and underpins all 6G spectrum strategy decisions.

Annexure C

6G Multi-Layer Spectrum Orchestration Model

6G spectrum strategy is predicated on a fundamental shift in design philosophy: from **spectrum dominance** where a single superior band is sought to **spectrum diversity**, where multiple bands coexist under intelligent orchestration. Each frequency tier fulfils a distinct architectural role, and the orchestration layer binds them into a coherent, user-transparent service fabric.

1

Sub-6 GHz

Baseline ubiquitous coverage the foundational connectivity layer ensuring no user is left unserved.

2

Mid-Band

Balanced performance tier primary carrier for most urban and suburban traffic with acceptable range and high throughput.

3

mmWave

Hotspot capacity layer dense indoor and event environments where extreme throughput density is required.

4

THz

Ultra-high throughput for proximity links, backhaul, and sensing-communication integrated applications.

5

NTN

Resilience and global reach seamless service continuity in maritime, rural, and disaster-affected zones.

> **Key Insight: Spectrum diversity replaces spectrum dominance.** The enabling technologies AI-driven allocation, beamforming, RIS, and dynamic spectrum sharing are the orchestration engines that make coexistence operationally viable.

Enabling Technologies

Technologies Underpinning Spectrum Orchestration

AI-Driven Allocation

Machine learning models continuously predict traffic demand, interference patterns, and mobility trajectories to pre-position spectrum resources before congestion occurs. Reinforcement learning agents operate at sub-second timescales across all frequency tiers simultaneously.

Beamforming

Spatial multiplexing via adaptive beamforming concentrates energy precisely toward intended receivers, suppressing interference and extending effective range at higher frequencies where path loss is severe.

Reconfigurable Intelligent Surfaces

RIS panels reshape the propagation environment by reflecting, refracting, and phase-shifting incident signals effectively extending mmWave and sub-THz coverage beyond line-of-sight constraints without active RF chains.

Dynamic Spectrum Sharing

Real-time coexistence mechanisms allow multiple RATs and frequency users to share spectrum under centralised interference coordination, maximising spectral efficiency across heterogeneous deployment scenarios.

Cell-Free MIMO: Mathematical Model and Advantages

The received signal at user *k* in a cell-free system is the coherent superposition of signals from all *L* distributed access points, each contributing through their respective channel gain. The simplified received signal model is expressed as:

$$y_k = \sum_{l=1}^{L} h_{lk} \cdot x_l + n_k$$

Where **hlk** denotes the channel gain between AP *l* and user *k*, **xl** is the transmitted signal from AP *l*, and **nk** represents additive noise. The key performance gain arises from joint precoding across all *L* access points effectively converting inter-cell interference into constructive signal energy.

Uniform QoS

All users experience comparable signal quality regardless of physical position eliminating the cell-edge performance penalty endemic to cellular systems.

Reduced Interference

Cooperative transmission converts inter-AP interference into coherent signal gain through joint precoding, fundamentally changing the interference regime.

Seamless Mobility

User-centric AP association updates continuously without discrete handover events, eliminating latency spikes during mobility transitions.

Key Insight: In cell-free MIMO, **performance scales with cooperation not infrastructure density alone.** The cooperation gain can exceed the benefit of simply deploying more isolated base stations.

Annexure E

6G Use Case Technical Requirements

6G must simultaneously support a diverse set of verticals whose performance requirements are not merely demanding in isolation they are heterogeneous and often contradictory. A network slice serving extended reality must deliver sub-millisecond latency alongside multi-Gbps throughput, while an Industry 5.0 control loop demands deterministic jitter-free delivery over sustained periods. The air interface, slicing architecture, and resource scheduler must resolve these competing demands in real time.

Use Case	Latency	Reliability	Data Rate	Key Driver
Extended Reality (XR)	<1 ms	Ultra-high	Multi-Gbps	Immersion
Autonomous Vehicles	<1 ms	Ultra-reliable	High	Safety
Industry 5.0	<1 ms	Deterministic	Medium	Control
Remote Healthcare	<1 ms	Mission-critical	High	Precision

> **Key Insight:** 6G must support **heterogeneous requirements simultaneously** not sequentially across dedicated deployments. This demands a network architecture that is polymorphic by design.

Use Case Deep Dive: Performance Constraints

Extended Reality (XR)

XR demands sub-1 ms motion-to-photon latency to prevent vestibular mismatch. At multi-Gbps throughput, holographic streaming requires sustained air interface capacity that rivals fixed fibre in reliability.

Autonomous Vehicles

V2X communication safety-critical messages must be delivered with <1 ms latency and >99.9999% reliability. Even a single packet loss during emergency manoeuvring has life-safety implications.

Industry 5.0

Closed-loop industrial control requires deterministic, jitter-free delivery not just low average latency. Tail latency bounds of microseconds are necessary for synchronised multi-robot coordination.

Remote Healthcare

Teleoperated surgery and real-time diagnostic imaging require mission-critical reliability. Network failures are clinically unacceptable the air interface must provide five-nines availability as a baseline.

Annexure F

Energy Efficiency and Sustainability

Energy efficiency is not merely an operational cost concern for 6G it is a scalability constraint. The combination of AI-driven compute workloads, dense infrastructure deployment, and the inherently poor power efficiency of THz-band hardware creates an energy demand profile that, without active mitigation, would render 6G economically and environmentally inviable at scale.

Challenges

- **High compute demand** AI inference at the RAN edge is power-intensive, particularly for large model inference at sub-ms deadlines
- **Dense infrastructure** cell-free and small-cell deployments multiply the number of active radio nodes per km^2
- **THz inefficiencies** power amplifier efficiency at sub-THz frequencies remains poor, increasing energy per transmitted bit

Solutions

- **AI-driven energy optimisation** predictive traffic models enable proactive resource scaling, minimising idle-state power consumption
- **Sleep modes for network nodes** dynamic node deactivation during low-traffic periods with AI-managed wake cycles
- **Green networking protocols** energy-aware routing, joint computation-communication optimisation, and renewable energy integration across edge infrastructure

Key Insight: Energy efficiency will define the scalability of 6G. Architectural choices made today from hardware selection to AI model size will determine whether 6G's energy footprint is sustainable at global deployment scale.

Metrics

Energy Efficiency: Generation-on-Generation Trajectory

The following chart illustrates the relative energy consumption per gigabit transmitted across mobile network generations, indexed against a 4G LTE baseline of 100. 5G improved efficiency through massive MIMO gain and sleep mode standardisation. 6G targets a further order-of-magnitude reduction through AI-native energy management though this target requires substantial hardware and protocol innovation to achieve.

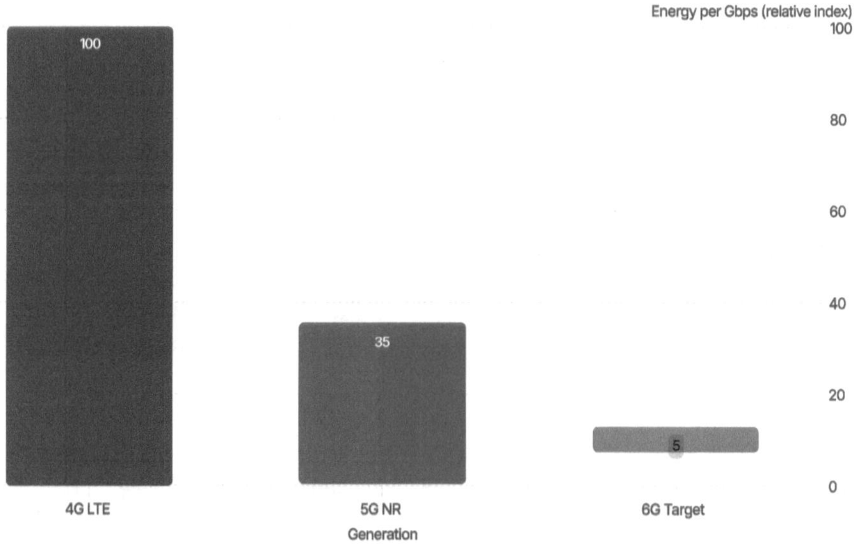

Achieving the 6G energy efficiency target requires co-design of AI inference hardware, RF front-ends, and protocol stacks treating energy as a first-order system resource alongside latency and throughput.

Annexure G

Standards and Ecosystem Overview

6G standardisation is proceeding in parallel with technology research an intentional structural shift from prior generations where standards followed deployments. The objective is to ensure that architectural principles such as AI nativity, spectrum flexibility, and security-by-design are embedded in the standard from its foundation, rather than retrofitted. Four bodies currently dominate the global 6G standards landscape.

3GPP

The primary radio access and core network standards body. 6G work items are expected to begin formal study phases post-Release 18/19, building on 5G-Advanced foundations.

ITU-R

Responsible for IMT-2030 framework definition establishing the high-level vision, spectrum identification, and capability requirements that national regulators and 3GPP must align with.

Hexa-X

EU-funded flagship 6G research initiative coordinating technology research across industry and academia. Focused on AI-native air interface, sub-THz, and joint communication-sensing architectures.

Next G Alliance

North American industry-led initiative under the Alliance for Telecommunications Industry Solutions (ATIS), focusing on national 6G roadmapping, spectrum policy, and supply chain priorities.

Annexure G
Standards Focus Areas Driving 6G Design

AI-Native Networks

Standardising interfaces and protocols for AI models operating natively within the network including model training data exchange between nodes, inference result sharing, and AI lifecycle management across the control plane.

Spectrum Standardisation

Harmonising global frequency allocations across sub-6 GHz, mid-band, mmWave, and sub-THz bands critical for enabling device roaming, interference management, and coordinated deployments across regulatory jurisdictions.

Interoperability

Defining open interfaces between vendor equipment particularly for disaggregated RAN architectures to prevent proprietary lock-in and enable multi-vendor deployments at scale across the cell-free MIMO and O-RAN paradigms.

Security Frameworks

Embedding zero-trust principles, post-quantum cryptography readiness, and AI-assisted threat detection into the standard ensuring security is a native property of the architecture rather than an overlay service.

Key Insight: 6G will be shaped as much by **standards as by technology**. The decisions made in standards bodies today will constrain or enable every deployment choice for the next decade.

Annexure H

Implementation Challenges

The technical case for 6G is well-established. The implementation challenge translating validated research into global-scale operational networks is where most prior-generation programmes encountered their most significant friction. 6G compounds these challenges through the unprecedented scope of its technical ambitions: AI-native operation, THz hardware, cell-free geometry, and NTN integration must all mature simultaneously and interoperable.

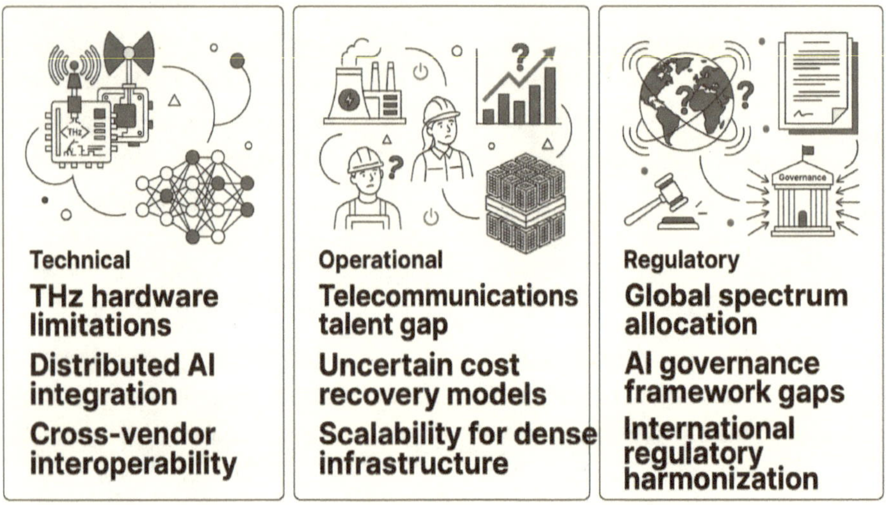

Technical Challenges

Technical Implementation Barriers

Hardware Limitations

Sub-THz and THz-band hardware power amplifiers, low-noise amplifiers, and integrated antenna arrays remains far from the performance and cost targets required for mass deployment. Semiconductor process nodes capable of efficient operation above 100 GHz are still maturing, with power efficiency remaining a primary constraint. CMOS scaling alone is insufficient; novel compound semiconductor materials and packaging architectures are required.

AI Integration Complexity

Embedding AI models across a distributed network from RAN nodes to cloud core introduces questions of model consistency, training data provenance, inference latency budgets, and fault behaviour when AI predictions are incorrect. Standardised AI lifecycle management interfaces do not yet exist at the required granularity, and the interaction between AI agents operating at different timescales remains poorly characterised.

Interoperability

Multi-vendor cell-free MIMO deployments require open, low-latency fronthaul interfaces between distributed APs and centralised processing units. Achieving the cooperative gains modelled in theory while preserving interoperability across vendors demands interface specifications that are simultaneously open and performance-preserving a tension not yet fully resolved in 5G O-RAN deployments.

Operational Challenges

Operational and Deployment Barriers

Talent Gap

6G requires a workforce fluent in both telecommunications engineering and machine learning a combination that is currently scarce. University curricula have not yet converged on an AI-native networking discipline, and the lead time for developing this expertise at industry scale is measured in years, not months. Operators and vendors must begin workforce development programmes well before commercial deployments commence.

Cost Models

The capital expenditure profile for 6G dense distributed antenna deployment, AI compute infrastructure at the edge, and NTN integration is significantly higher than 5G. Current revenue models for telecommunications operators do not clearly support this investment level. New value capture mechanisms, including network-as-a-service for enterprise verticals and compute-as-a-service at the edge, must mature before business cases close.

Deployment Scalability

Cell-free massive MIMO requires orders of magnitude more physical installation points than traditional macro-cell deployments. Site acquisition, power provisioning, fibre backhaul extension, and ongoing maintenance for thousands of distributed access points per km^2 represent a logistical challenge that exceeds prior network build programmes in complexity and duration.

Regulatory Challenges

Regulatory and Governance Barriers

> **Key Insight:** The biggest barrier to 6G is not technology it is **execution at scale**. Technical feasibility has been demonstrated across most domains; the rate-limiting factor is the convergence of standards, regulation, economics, and operational capability.

Annexure Summary: Key Insights Consolidated

The eight annexures collectively establish the technical substrate upon which 6G system design must be grounded. Each insight stands independently, but together they define the irreducible constraints and opportunities that every 6G architect must internalise.

01

A — Architecture

6G is not a layered system intelligence is woven across all domains simultaneously.

02

B — Spectrum Physics

No single band meets all requirements multi-layer orchestration is mandatory.

03

C — Spectrum Strategy

Spectrum diversity replaces spectrum dominance as the governing design philosophy.

04

D — Cell-Free MIMO

Performance scales with cooperation not infrastructure density alone.

05

E — Use Cases

6G must support heterogeneous, simultaneous requirements across all verticals.

06

F — Energy

Energy efficiency will define the scalability and viability of 6G at global scale.

07

G — Standards

6G will be shaped as much by standards decisions as by technology breakthroughs.

08

H — Execution

The greatest barrier to 6G is not technology it is execution at scale.

ANNEXURE: I

Futuristic Communication Paradigms

Beyond 6G: Redefining the Nature of Communication

From the telegraph to 5G, every leap in communication technology has optimised the same three constraints: **distance, medium, and delay**. What emerges next transcends these parameters entirely transforming communication from data exchange into the seamless alignment of intelligence across distributed systems.

Introduction: Beyond Transmission

Communication has always been constrained by three fundamental dimensions: **distance, medium, and delay**. Each generation from wired telegraphy to 5G has incrementally optimised these constraints. However, the emerging paradigm of intelligent networks challenges the very foundation of this model.

As intelligence becomes embedded within infrastructure, communication is no longer limited to data exchange. Instead, it evolves into **state synchronisation, intent sharing, and cognitive interaction.**

> The next era of communication will not be defined by how fast we transmit data but by how seamlessly systems align intelligence.

Contextual Understanding
Grasping the environment and user needs.

Shared Ontologies
Establishing common language and structure.

Adaptive Protocols
Creating flexible rules for interaction.

Trust and Transparency
Building confidence through open processes.

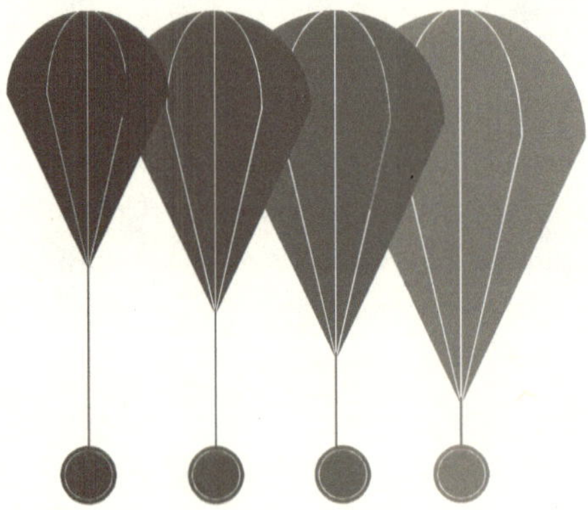

Ten Paradigms Redefining Communication

This document explores ten radical conceptual frameworks that will shape the next frontier of networked intelligence from quantum-inspired state synchronisation to communication without a medium.

From Transmission to Entanglement

State synchronisation replaces packet exchange

Intent-Based Communication

Networks interpret outcomes, not commands

Semantic Communication Networks

Meaning supersedes bit-level transmission

Brain–Network Interfaces

Direct neural interaction with infrastructure

Holographic Reality Synchronisation

Shared presence across distributed nodes

Swarm Communication Systems

Decentralised, emergent intelligence networks

Zero-Latency Illusion Systems

Prediction-based elimination of perceived delay

Interplanetary Communication Models

Anticipation-driven deep-space networking

Consciousness-Aware Communication

Adaptive systems attuned to cognitive state

Communication Without Medium

The radical elimination of transmission itself

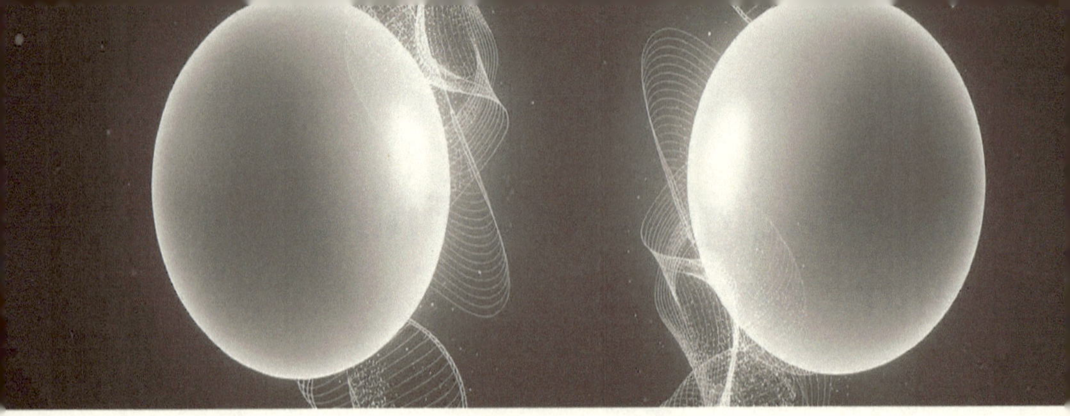

PARADIGM 1

From Transmission to Entanglement

Traditional communication follows a deterministic linear pipeline: **Encode → Transmit → Decode.** Future systems may fundamentally abandon this architecture in favour of **state synchronisation models**, where distributed systems maintain consistent shared states without explicit packet exchange.

Drawing analogies from quantum entanglement, distributed databases with eventual consistency, and blockchain state replication, these architectures treat communication not as message-passing but as convergence of shared truth.

State Synchronisation: Operational Architecture

Encode
Prepare payload for transmission

Transmit
Send data across channels

Decode
Reconstruct received payload

Shared State
Maintain common state vectors

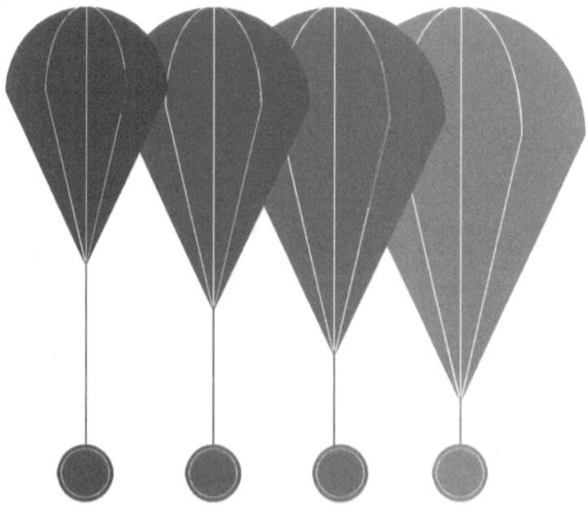

In the state synchronisation model, systems maintain shared state vectors that propagate updates through event-driven mechanisms rather than scheduled transmissions. Communication becomes **state convergence** a fundamentally different information-theoretic paradigm.

Technical Analogies

- Quantum entanglement correlated states
- Distributed databases eventual consistency
- Blockchain state replication across nodes

System Implications

- Ultra-low latency perception
- Reduced bandwidth requirements
- Resilient distributed architectures

Key Insight: Communication shifts from "sending information" to "aligning system states."

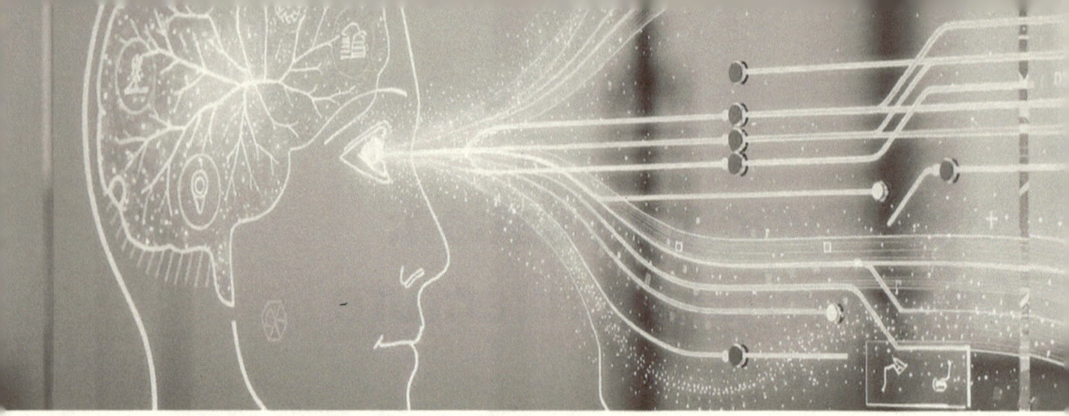

PARADIGM 2

Intent-Based Communication

In current networks, instructions are explicit and rigid every action must be precisely specified. Future systems evolve toward **intent abstraction**, where systems define desired outcomes rather than execution steps. The network becomes an intelligent interpreter, not a passive conduit.

This paradigm shift redistributes cognitive load from the user to the infrastructure, enabling autonomous, context-aware decision-making at network scale.

Intent Architecture: From Command to Outcome

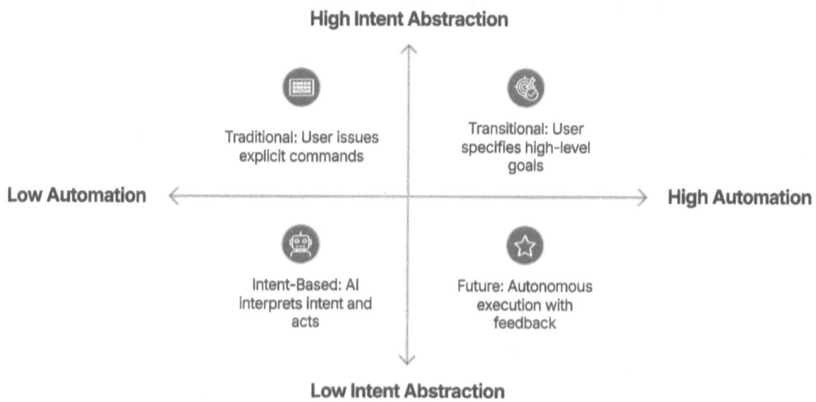

Advantages

→ **Reduced signalling overhead**

Fewer explicit instructions traversing the network

→ **Adaptive optimisation**

Systems self-tune to contextual conditions

→ **Context-aware decisions**

Outcomes reflect environmental and user state

Challenges

→ **Ambiguity resolution**

Interpreting imprecise or conflicting intents

→ **Intent validation**

Ensuring interpreted actions match true desires

→ **Governance boundaries**

Defining limits of autonomous interpretation

> Networks will no longer execute commands they will interpret intent.

PARADIGM 3

Semantic Communication Networks

Shannon's foundational communication model optimises **bit transmission fidelity**. Future semantic communication systems reorient the optimisation target entirely: they optimise **semantic accuracy** ensuring the meaning conveyed is preserved, irrespective of the bit representation.

Rather than encoding and decoding raw data, semantic systems transfer the *essence* of information, leveraging AI models, edge intelligence, and knowledge graphs to reconstruct meaning at the receiver.

Semantic vs. Bit-Level Transmission

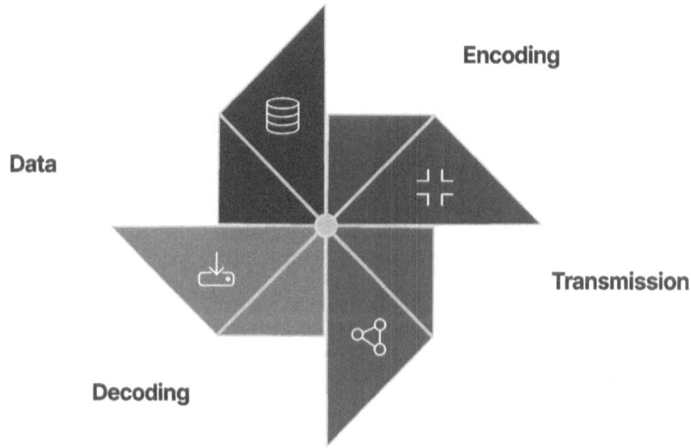

Key Enablers

Transformer Models & LLMs

Edge Intelligence

Knowledge Graphs

Target Applications

- **XR systems** immersive spatial communication
- **Autonomous networks** machine-to-machine meaning transfer
- **IoT ecosystems** compressed, meaningful sensor data

Key Insight: The most efficient communication system transmits meaning not data.

PARADIGM 4

Brain–Network Interfaces

The most intimate frontier in communication eliminates physical interfaces entirely, enabling **direct neural interaction with networks**. Brain signals, interpreted by AI, translate thought patterns into network actions collapsing the distance between cognition and computation.

From medical neuroprosthetics restoring lost function to augmented cognition systems extending human capability, brain–network interfaces represent both the pinnacle of human-centred design and its most profound ethical challenge.

BNI Architecture & Risk Landscape

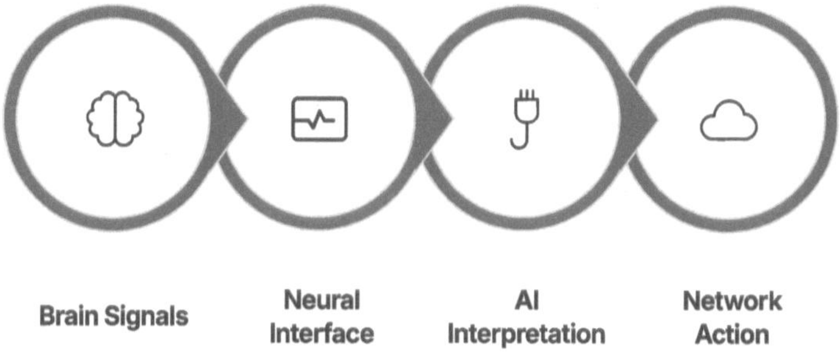

Applications

- Medical neuroprosthetics motor function restoration
- Augmented cognition memory and processing extension
- Immersive systems thought-driven spatial interaction

Critical Risks

- **Cognitive privacy** protection of neural data from surveillance
- **Signal manipulation** adversarial interference with neural signals
- **Ethical boundaries** consent, agency, and identity integrity

> **Key Insight:** When thoughts become signals, communication becomes instantaneous but deeply sensitive.

PARADIGM 5

Holographic Reality Synchronisation

Beyond discrete holograms, future systems will enable **shared spatial environments synchronised in real time** across geographically distributed nodes. Participants do not merely see each other they inhabit a common, dynamically rendered spatial context.

Achieving this demands a convergence of sub-millisecond latency, real-time spatial mapping, AI rendering engines, and distributed edge compute a formidable systems engineering challenge that redefines what "presence" means in networked communication.

Holographic Sync: Technical Requirements

Sub-Millisecond Latency

Target threshold of <1 ms end-to-end to ensure spatial coherence across all nodes simultaneously

Spatial Mapping

Continuous real-time reconstruction of physical environments for accurate shared rendering

AI Rendering Engines

Neural rendering pipelines that adapt fidelity dynamically based on available compute and bandwidth

Distributed Edge Compute

Processing pushed to the network edge to minimise round-trip delays and centralisation bottlenecks

> The future is not virtual communication it is shared presence.

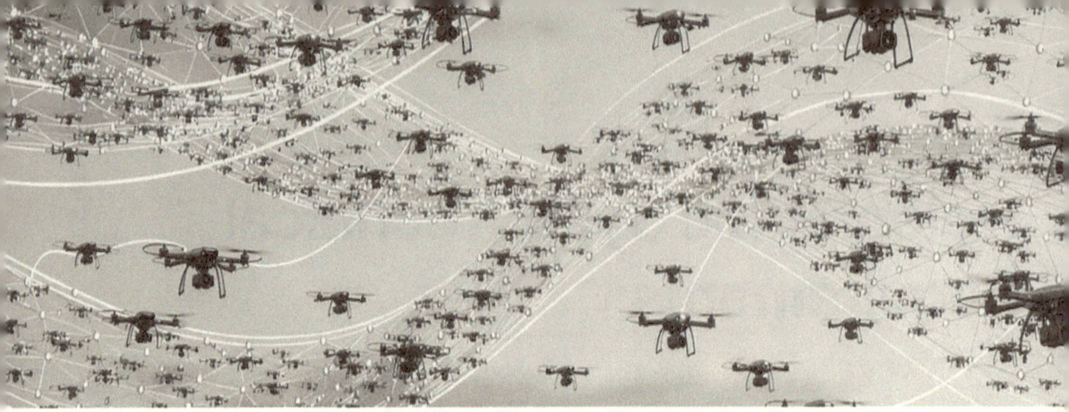

PARADIGM 6

Swarm Communication Systems

Inspired by biological systems ant colonies, murmuration of starlings, neural networks swarm communication architectures rely on **decentralisation, self-organisation, and emergent intelligence.** No central controller orchestrates the system; intelligence arises from local interactions.

This paradigm enables communication infrastructures that are inherently resilient, scalable, and adaptive capable of operating in environments where centralised architectures would catastrophically fail.

Swarm Architecture & Applications

Architectural Principle

Unlike hub-and-spoke topologies, swarm networks operate as a **fully distributed mesh:**

Node ↔ Node ↔ Node

No central controller. Emergent coordination from peer interactions.

Core Properties

- Decentralisation no single point of failure
- Self-organisation adaptive topology formation
- Emergent intelligence macro-behaviour from micro-rules

Application Domains

Drone Swarms

Coordinated aerial surveillance, delivery, and infrastructure inspection

Sensor Networks

Environmental monitoring at massive scale with local data processing

Nano-Scale Systems

Intra-body medical nanobots communicating without central control

Key Insight: Future networks will behave less like machines and more like living systems.

PARADIGM 7

Zero-Latency Illusion Systems

Physical zero latency is an impossibility constrained by the speed of light. Yet future systems can engineer **perceived zero latency** through sophisticated prediction, pre-rendering, and edge caching mechanisms that anticipate user actions before they are consciously made.

The engineering challenge shifts from reducing propagation delay to **accurately modelling future states** a fundamentally different problem space that blends communications theory with probabilistic AI.

> The future of communication is not eliminating delay but eliminating its perception.

Latency Masking: The Prediction Triad

Predictive Modelling

AI-driven anticipation of next actions, states, and requests based on behavioural and contextual signals enabling pre-computation of likely outcomes before the trigger event occurs

Pre-Rendering

Prospective frame and scene generation at the edge, so visual output is ready to display before the user's intent is fully transmitted to the source

Edge Caching

Probabilistic placement of anticipated content at the network edge, collapsing effective retrieval latency to near-instantaneous local access times

PARADIGM 8

Interplanetary Communication Models

Communication beyond Earth introduces an entirely different operational reality: propagation delays measured in **minutes to hours**, not milliseconds. The Earth–Mars round-trip delay ranges from approximately 6 to 44 minutes depending on orbital alignment making real-time interaction physically impossible.

This necessitates a complete rethinking of communication architecture, shifting from reactive to **anticipation-driven, asynchronous, and autonomous** operational models.

Deep-Space Networking Architecture

Core Challenges

- **High latency** 3 to 22 minutes one-way to Mars
- **Asynchronous operation** no synchronous handshake possible
- **Signal degradation** power loss over interplanetary distances

Enabling Solutions

1 **Delay-Tolerant Networking (DTN)**

Store-carry-forward architecture tolerating link disruptions and extreme delays

2 **Predictive Scheduling**

Pre-planned transmission windows based on orbital mechanics and contact prediction

3 **Autonomous Nodes**

Self-directing spacecraft and surface assets operating independently between Earth contacts

> Communication across space is not real-time it is anticipation-driven.

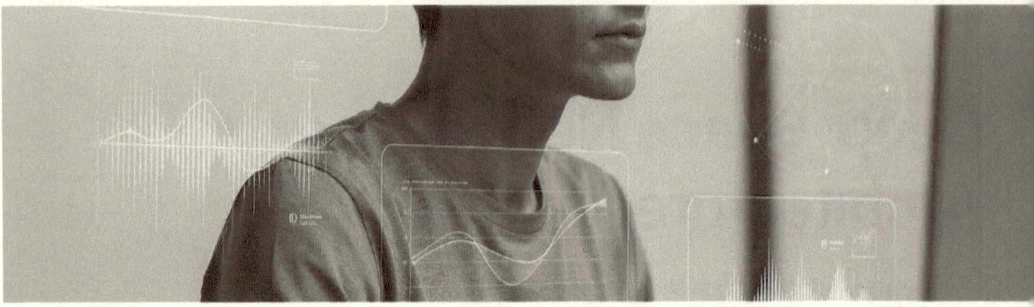

PARADIGM 9

Consciousness-Aware Communication

The ultimate personalisation frontier: systems that adapt communication modalities, information density, and interaction rhythms dynamically based on a user's real-time **emotional state, attentional capacity, and cognitive load.**

Rather than forcing humans to adapt to network protocols, consciousness-aware systems continuously sense and model the human cognitive state, adjusting every interaction parameter to optimise comprehension, reduce friction, and maintain engagement without overload.

> The ultimate interface may not be devices but awareness itself.

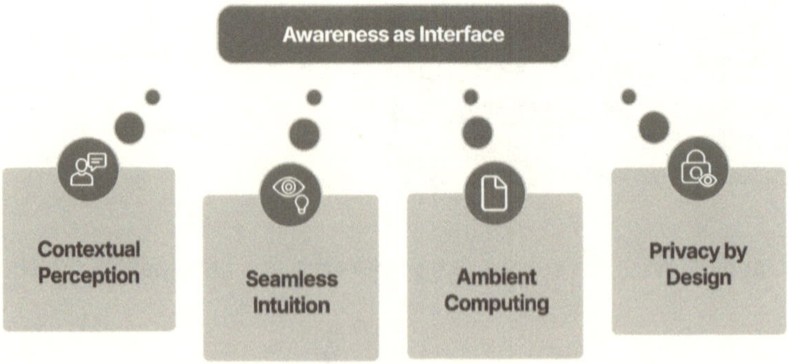

Cognitive State Adaptive Loop

Emotional State

Stress, calm, arousal mapped via biometric and behavioural signals to tune content delivery pace

Attention Level

Focus depth determines information density and interaction complexity offered by the system

Cognitive Load

Working memory saturation signals the system to simplify, defer, or restructure information flow

PARADIGM 10

Communication Without Medium

The most radical concept in this compendium: **communication without transmission**. If distributed intelligence achieves sufficient synchronisation through shared models, continuous state alignment, and ambient context sharing, the discrete act of "sending a message" may become vestigial.

This is not science fiction it is the logical extrapolation of trends in federated learning, shared world models, and ambient intelligence. Systems that have already converged on the same understanding require no further exchange to act in harmony.

The Mediumless Paradigm

NO CHANNEL

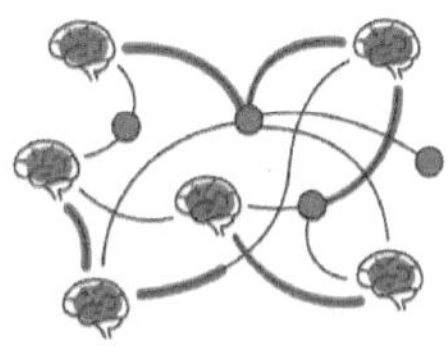

Distributed intelligence shares state directly.

NO DELAY

Continuous synchronization, not triggered events.

SHARED INTELLIGENCE

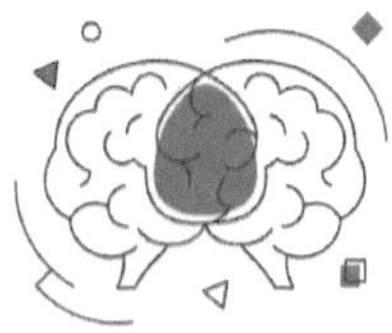

Systems converge on a single, common model.

> **Key Insight:** The final evolution of communication may eliminate communication itself replaced by the continuous, silent alignment of distributed intelligence.

This concept unifies all preceding paradigms: state synchronisation, intent abstraction, semantic transfer, and cognitive awareness converge into a single emergent property **intelligence that does not need to communicate because it has already aligned**.

Reflection: Open Questions for the Field

These ten paradigms raise profound questions that extend beyond engineering into philosophy, ethics, and the nature of cognition itself. They demand engagement not only from network architects but from ethicists, cognitive scientists, and policymakers.

Can meaning fully replace data?

Is semantic fidelity achievable without information loss, or does compression of meaning introduce irreducible ambiguity?

Will communication merge with cognition?

As brain–network interfaces mature, where does thinking end and transmitting begin?

Can systems align without transmission?

What is the theoretical minimum information exchange required for two systems to achieve shared understanding?

What defines communication in an intelligent ecosystem?

If aligned AI systems act in concert without messaging, has communication occurred or has it been transcended?

Closing Statement

We began by sending signals across wires. We evolved to transmitting data across the world at the speed of light. Each generation optimised the channel making it faster, wider, more reliable.

The paradigms explored in this document suggest a different trajectory entirely: **a future in which the channel itself becomes unnecessary**. Not because transmission has been perfected, but because intelligence has been sufficiently distributed that alignment precedes the need to communicate.

> We began by sending signals across wires. The future may not involve transmission at all but the seamless alignment of intelligence across systems.

Past	Present	Future
Signals across wires optimising the channel	Global data transmission optimising throughput and latency	Intelligence alignment transcending transmission itself

ANNEXURE: J

Interplanetary Communication Networks

Architecture, Routing, and Autonomous Operation Beyond Earth Orbit

As human activity expands toward the Moon, Mars, and deep space, traditional terrestrial and satellite communication paradigms become fundamentally insufficient. This concept paper presents a reference architecture for interplanetary communication networks, extending 6G non-terrestrial network principles toward post-6G (7G-class) systems analysing routing challenges, autonomous delay-tolerant mechanisms, and enabling technologies including optical links, quantum security, and AI-driven network control.

Abstract & Keywords

Extreme propagation delays, intermittent connectivity, orbital dynamics, and harsh physical environments demand a fundamentally new networking model. This paper proposes a conceptual architecture for interplanetary communication networks, positioning them as the outermost frontier of future communication evolution.

We analyse routing challenges, propose autonomous delay-tolerant mechanisms, and outline enabling technologies that form the foundation of sustainable interplanetary connectivity a system that must operate without real-time human intervention across distances spanning hundreds of millions of kilometres.

Keywords

- Interplanetary Communication
- Deep Space Networking
- Delay-Tolerant Networking
- 6G / 7G Architecture
- Optical Communication
- Quantum Communication
- Autonomous Routing

1. Introduction

The evolution of communication networks from terrestrial cellular systems to satellite-based non-terrestrial networks (NTN) marks a critical step toward global connectivity. However, extending communication beyond Earth orbit introduces challenges that exceed the design assumptions of current 5G and emerging 6G architectures.

Speed-of-Light Latency

Physical propagation limits impose irreducible one-way delays of seconds to tens of minutes.

Discontinuous Connectivity

Orbital mechanics create predictable but unavoidable communication blackouts.

Autonomous Decision-Making

No real-time human correction is possible networks must self-govern.

Extreme Reliability

Mission-critical systems depend on communication infrastructure with no tolerance for failure.

2. Fundamental Constraints: Distance & Latency

Real-time feedback, acknowledgements, and centralised control are physically infeasible across interplanetary distances. The speed of light imposes hard lower bounds on every communication exchange a constraint that no technological advance can overcome.

Link	One-Way Latency	Implication
Earth – Moon	~1.3 seconds	Near-real-time feasible with buffering
Earth – Mars (closest approach)	~3 minutes	Interactive sessions impossible
Earth – Mars (farthest separation)	~22 minutes	Full autonomous operation required
Earth – Jupiter	~35–52 minutes	Store-and-forward only
Earth – Deep Space Probe	Hours to days	Asynchronous batch transmission

Round-trip times are double the one-way figures above. A command sent to a Mars surface rover during maximum separation will not receive a response for over 44 minutes rendering Earth-based teleoperation operationally untenable.

3. Interplanetary Network Architecture

A layered reference architecture organises interplanetary communication into four functional planes, each addressing a distinct set of constraints. This abstraction enables modular design, independent evolution of each layer, and clear fault isolation boundaries.

1

Physical Layer

Optical laser links · RF backup · Quantum channels

2

Transport Layer

DTN bundle protocol · Store-and-forward · Custody transfer

3

Autonomous Control Layer

AI routing · Orbital prediction · Fault recovery

4

Application Layer

Telemetry · Human comms · Navigation · Science data

Each layer is designed to operate independently in the event of upper-layer failure, ensuring physical connectivity persists even when higher-level protocols are disrupted by radiation events, hardware faults, or software anomalies.

4. Interplanetary Routing Model

4.1 Store-and-Forward DTN Routing

Unlike terrestrial IP routing, interplanetary routing employs Delay/Disruption Tolerant Networking (DTN). Data bundles are transmitted opportunistically during available contact windows, stored at intermediate relay nodes for minutes or hours, then forwarded when the next link becomes available. Acknowledgements may arrive tens of minutes after initial transmission.

4.2 Autonomous Predictive Routing

Routing decisions are computed from orbital mechanics models, not instantaneous link state. An onboard Orbital Prediction Engine forecasts link availability windows, identifies optimal transmission slots, and autonomously selects routes without Earth-based intervention. This predictive approach is fundamentally different from reactive terrestrial routing protocols such as OSPF or BGP.

Source Node

Transmit when contact window opens

Relay Orbiter

Store data for minutes or hours

Deep Space Gateway

Forward when orbital alignment is available

Destination Node

Receive and acknowledge asynchronously

4.3 Interplanetary Mesh Topology

Each node in the interplanetary mesh acts simultaneously as a router, storage buffer, and relay. The topology spans cislunar space, the Earth–Mars corridor, and deep space relay infrastructure forming a resilient, self-organising network capable of surviving individual node failures.

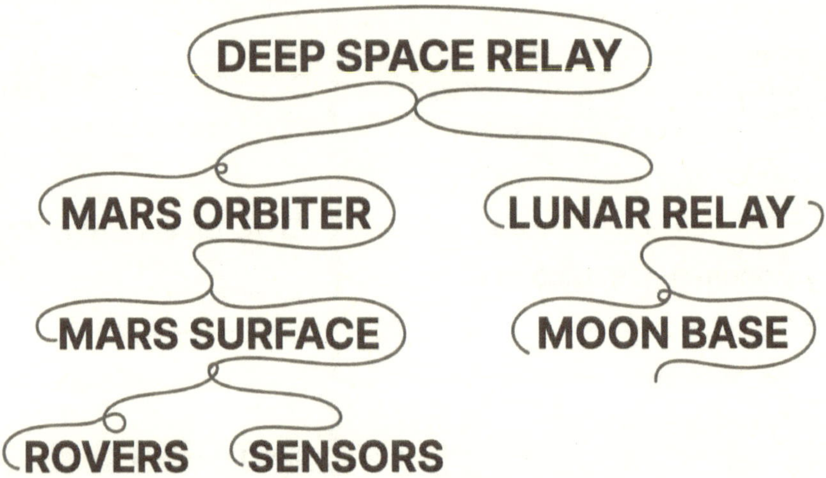

Topology is inherently dynamic orbital motion continuously reshapes link availability, requiring the network to re-optimise routing schedules on a rolling basis using pre-computed contact graphs derived from mission trajectory data.

5. Optical and Quantum Communication Integration

5.1 Optical Backbone

Free-space optical (FSO) laser links form the primary high-throughput backbone of the interplanetary network. Operating at near-infrared wavelengths, these links offer data rates orders of magnitude beyond conventional RF systems. The trade-off is extreme pointing accuracy requirements sub-microradian beam alignment across planetary distances and vulnerability to solar conjunction and atmospheric distortion at terminal stations.

- Extremely high throughput vs. RF alternatives
- Narrow beamwidth demands precision gimbal systems
- Earth–Moon–Mars relay chain enables multi-hop optical paths

5.2 Quantum-Secured Control Channels

Navigation commands, life-support uplinks, and mission-critical telemetry traverse quantum key distribution (QKD) channels layered over the optical backbone. QKD provides information-theoretic security guarantees that remain valid even against future quantum computing adversaries a non-negotiable property for commands that control autonomous spacecraft and surface systems operating beyond Earth orbit.

- QKD over optical links for command channel security
- Distributed key caches at relay nodes for latency tolerance
- Quantum-safe algorithms as fallback during solar events

6. Fault Tolerance and Self-Healing

Interplanetary networks must survive node failure entirely without human intervention. The round-trip communication delay to even the nearest planetary node renders Earth-based fault response operationally meaningless by the time a fault notification arrives at Earth and a corrective command returns, the affected mission window may have closed irreversibly.

Autonomous Recovery Requirements

- Sub-second local fault detection via watchdog telemetry
- Pre-computed alternate contact schedules loaded at each node
- Custody transfer ensures no data loss during node failover

Design Philosophy

- Each node is a fully autonomous communication entity
- No single point of failure may be mission-critical
- Recovery logic executes locally without Earth acknowledgement

7. Energy-Aware Routing

Energy scarcity is a defining constraint of deep space communication nodes. Solar irradiance diminishes with the square of distance from the Sun a node at Mars receives less than 43% of the solar power available at Earth orbit. Nuclear and radioisotope power sources supplement solar generation but are mass-constrained.

1

Solar Availability Assessment

Compute real-time energy budget from irradiance models and battery state

2

Transmission Priority Assignment

Rank data queues by mission criticality and link window timing

3

Opportunistic Data Transfer

Transmit only when energy-positive; defer non-critical bundles autonomously

8. Security and Governance

Threat Model

- Command spoofing targeting autonomous surface systems
- Relay node compromise via supply-chain or physical access
- Signal interception during predictable transmission windows
- Replay attacks exploiting high-latency acknowledgement gaps

Required Controls

- **Quantum-safe encryption** post-quantum cryptographic algorithms across all link types
- **Distributed trust anchors** decentralised certificate authority chains resilient to single-point compromise
- **International governance frameworks** spectrum allocation, orbital slot coordination, and shared infrastructure treaties

Interplanetary communication infrastructure must be globally governed rather than nationally isolated. Sovereign ownership of relay nodes creates single points of political failure in mission-critical paths.

9. Relationship to 6G and 7G Evolution

Interplanetary networking is not a separate research domain it is the logical extension of the 6G evolutionary trajectory. Each generation extends the reach and autonomy of the network; interplanetary systems represent the endpoint of that progression.

5G	6G	7G
Terrestrial broadband, eMBB, URLLC, mMTC. Earth-surface coverage with centralised core.	Global coverage including NTN, AI-native control, sub-THz links, and integrated sensing.	Planetary and interplanetary cognitive networks. Fully autonomous, delay-tolerant, quantum-secured.

The transition from 6G to 7G-class interplanetary networks is not merely incremental it requires a categorical shift from reactive, connection-oriented protocols to predictive, store-and-forward autonomous architectures operating across timescales incompatible with human-in-the-loop control.

10. Open Research Challenges

1 **Autonomous Routing Protocols**

Standardised interplanetary routing protocols capable of operating across heterogeneous node types, power profiles, and mission-specific constraints without Earth-based coordination.

2 **Optical–Quantum Hybrid Switching**

Seamless integration of high-throughput FSO data channels with low-rate QKD key distribution over shared optical infrastructure with dynamic wavelength management.

3 **Planetary Digital Twins**

High-fidelity simulation environments modelling orbital mechanics, link availability, and node behaviour to enable pre-mission protocol validation and real-time routing prediction.

4 **Bio-Integrated Astronaut Communication**

Low-power, body-area network integration enabling continuous physiological monitoring and high-bandwidth crew communications across the full interplanetary network stack.

5 **Long-Term Governance Models**

International legal and technical frameworks governing spectrum use, relay node ownership, data sovereignty, and emergency priority access across multi-agency, multi-national missions.

11. Conclusion

> The future of communication does not end at Earth's atmosphere. It begins beyond it.

Interplanetary communication represents the most extreme operating environment for communication systems ever conceived. It demands autonomy, intelligence, security, and resilience beyond any terrestrial precedent. The constraints are not engineering inconveniences they are fundamental physical realities that require a categorical departure from the design assumptions underlying every prior generation of communication network.

As humanity moves toward sustained extraterrestrial presence on the Moon, Mars, and beyond, communication networks will evolve from support systems into mission-critical planetary infrastructure. The architecture presented in this paper provides a conceptual foundation for that evolution, bridging 6G NTN principles toward a 7G-class interplanetary communication paradigm.

Autonomous

Self-governing without real-time Earth intervention

Delay-Tolerant

Store-and-forward across multi-minute propagation paths

Quantum-Secured

Information-theoretic security for mission-critical channels

Globally Governed

International frameworks transcending national boundaries

References / Bibliography

A comprehensive bibliography of standards, industry reports, academic research, and thought leadership underpinning the study of 6G, wireless evolution, AI-native networks, semantic communications, security, edge computing, and future communication paradigms.

Standards, Industry Reports & Academic Research

A. Standards and Industry Reports

[1] International Telecommunication Union, *"IMT-2030 (6G) Framework and Overall Objectives of the Future Development of IMT,"* ITU-R, Geneva, Switzerland, 2023.

[2] 3rd Generation Partnership Project, *"Study on 6G Network Architecture,"* TR 38.xxx (Draft), 2024.

[3] Next G Alliance, *"6G Roadmap and Vision,"* ATIS, 2022.

[4] Hexa-X Project, *"6G Vision and Key Technologies,"* European Commission, 2021.

[5] GSMA, *"Mobile Economy Report 2023,"* GSMA Intelligence, 2023.

B. Academic Research (6G and Wireless Evolution)

[6] T. S. Rappaport et al., *"Wireless Communications and Applications Above 100 GHz: Opportunities and Challenges for 6G and Beyond,"* IEEE Access, vol. 7, pp. 78729–78757, 2019.

[7] M. Giordani et al., *"Toward 6G Networks: Use Cases and Technologies,"* IEEE Communications Magazine, vol. 58, no. 3, pp. 55–61, 2020.

[8] W. Saad et al., *"A Vision of 6G Wireless Systems: Applications, Trends, Technologies, and Open Research Problems,"* IEEE Network, vol. 34, no. 3, pp. 134–142, 2020.

[9] Y. Liu et al., *"Reconfigurable Intelligent Surfaces: Principles and Opportunities,"* IEEE Communications Surveys & Tutorials, vol. 23, no. 3, pp. 1546–1577, 2021.

[10] H. Tataria et al., *"6G Wireless Systems: Vision, Requirements, Challenges, Insights, and Opportunities,"* Proceedings of the IEEE, vol. 109, no. 7, pp. 1166–1199, 2021.

C. AI-Native Networks and Autonomous Systems

[11] LF Networking, *"Autonomous Networks and Zero-Touch Management,"* White Paper, 2022.

[12] European Telecommunications Standards Institute, *"Experiential Networked Intelligence (ENI): Use Cases,"* ETSI GS ENI 005, 2021.

[13] S. K. Sharma et al., *"Artificial Intelligence for 6G Networks,"* IEEE Wireless Communications, vol. 28, no. 6, pp. 8–15, 2021.

D. Semantic and Future Communication Paradigms

[14] E. C. Strinati et al., *"6G: The Next Frontier,"* IEEE Vehicular Technology Magazine, vol. 14, no. 3, pp. 42–50, 2019.

[15] D. Gunduz et al., *"Communicating with Semantic Information,"* IEEE Journal on Selected Areas in Communications, vol. 41, no. 1, pp. 1–18, 2023.

[16] DeepMind, *"Toward Neural Interfaces and General Intelligence,"* Research Insights, 2022.

Security, Edge Computing, Industry Leadership & Conceptual References

E. Security, Privacy, and Quantum Threats

[17] National Institute of Standards and Technology, *"Post-Quantum Cryptography Standardization,"* NIST, 2022.

[18] M. Mosca, *"Cybersecurity in an Era with Quantum Computers,"* IEEE Security & Privacy, vol. 16, no. 5, pp. 38–41, 2018.

[19] European Union Agency for Cybersecurity, *"Security for 5G and Beyond,"* ENISA Report, 2022.

F. Edge, Cloud, and Distributed Systems

[20] M. Satyanarayanan, *"The Emergence of Edge Computing,"* Computer, vol. 50, no. 1, pp. 30–39, 2017.

[21] NVIDIA, *"AI-RAN: Accelerating AI-Native Networks,"* Technical Brief, 2024.

G. Industry Thought Leadership and Strategic Outlook

[22] Nokia, *"6G Explained: From Vision to Reality,"* Nokia White Paper, 2023.

[23] Ericsson, *"6G: Connecting a Cyber-Physical World,"* Ericsson Technology Review, 2022.

[24] Huawei, *"6G Vision and Key Drivers,"* Huawei White Paper, 2021.

H. Additional Conceptual and Philosophical References

[25] J. Wheeler, *"Information, Physics, Quantum: The Search for Links,"* in Proceedings of the Third International Symposium on Foundations of Quantum Mechanics, 1989.

[26] W. Heisenberg, *Physics and Philosophy: The Revolution in Modern Science*, Harper & Row, 1958.

Glossary

Key Terms in 6G, AI-Native Networks, and Future Communication

A comprehensive reference guide covering the essential terminology across AI-native networks, 6G architecture, intelligent infrastructure, and next-generation communication paradigms.

A – F: Core Architecture & Foundational Concepts

AI-Native Network

A network where artificial intelligence is embedded across all layers (RAN, core, edge, and control plane), enabling autonomous decision-making and continuous optimization.

AI Control Plane

A layer in 6G architecture responsible for real-time monitoring, prediction, decision-making, and automated execution through closed-loop intelligence.

Autonomous Network

A self-operating network capable of sensing, deciding, and acting without continuous human intervention.

Beamforming

A signal processing technique that directs wireless signals toward specific users or devices rather than broadcasting in all directions.

Brain–Network Interface

A communication system enabling direct interaction between human neural signals and digital networks.

Cell-Free Network

A distributed wireless architecture where users are served by multiple coordinated access points without fixed cell boundaries.

Cognitive Infrastructure

A network system that integrates sensing, computation, and communication to make context-aware decisions.

Cloud-Native Core

A software-based core network architecture using microservices, APIs, and virtualization for flexibility and scalability.

Decision Layer

A conceptual layer in 6G where networks interpret intent, evaluate context, and autonomously execute actions.

Decision-as-a-Service (DaaS)

A business model where networks provide optimised outcomes or decisions rather than raw connectivity.

Digital Twin

A real-time digital replica of a physical system used for simulation, monitoring, and optimisation.

Edge Intelligence

Distributed AI capabilities deployed at the network edge to enable real-time decision-making with minimal latency.

Experiential Network

A network that adapts dynamically based on user experience, context, and intent rather than static configurations.

Frequency Band

A specific range of electromagnetic spectrum used for wireless communication (e.g., sub-6 GHz, mmWave, THz).

H – N: Advanced Capabilities & Network Paradigms

Holographic Communication

A form of immersive communication using 3D projections and real-time spatial interaction.

Intent-Based Networking

A paradigm where systems define desired outcomes instead of explicit instructions, allowing the network to determine optimal execution.

Integrated Sensing and Communication (ISAC)

A 6G capability where communication networks also perform sensing and environmental detection.

Interference Management

Techniques used to control and mitigate signal interference between wireless transmissions.

Latency

The time delay between sending and receiving data. Ultra-low latency is critical for real-time applications like autonomous systems.

Massive MIMO (Multiple Input Multiple Output)

A technology using large numbers of antennas to improve capacity, reliability, and signal quality.

Multi-Layer Spectrum Orchestration

The coordinated use of multiple frequency bands (sub-6 GHz, mmWave, THz) to optimise coverage and capacity.

Non-Terrestrial Network (NTN)

A communication network that includes satellites, aerial platforms, and space-based systems.

P – Z: Security, Intelligence & Emerging Technologies

Post-Quantum Cryptography (PQC)

Cryptographic techniques designed to remain secure against quantum computing attacks.

Predictive Network

A network capable of anticipating events and optimising resources before issues occur.

Quantum Communication

A communication method leveraging quantum mechanics principles such as entanglement for secure data transfer.

Reconfigurable Intelligent Surface (RIS)

A programmable surface that can dynamically control electromagnetic wave propagation to improve signal quality.

Semantic Communication

A communication approach focused on transmitting meaning rather than raw data.

Smart City

An urban environment that uses digital networks and data to optimise infrastructure, services, and sustainability.

Swarm Intelligence

A decentralised system where multiple entities cooperate to achieve collective behaviour without central control.

Terahertz (THz) Communication

High-frequency wireless communication offering extremely high data rates but limited coverage range.

Ultra-Reliable Low-Latency Communication (URLLC)

A communication requirement for mission-critical applications needing high reliability and minimal delay.

Zero Trust Architecture

A security framework where no entity is trusted by default, and all interactions are continuously verified.

Zero-Latency Perception

A system design approach where predictive techniques create the illusion of instantaneous response.

Epilogue

The Quiet Shift

There is a moment in every technological revolution that is easy to miss. It does not arrive with announcements. It does not declare itself as a turning point. It happens quietly a system becomes slightly more capable, a decision slightly faster, a process slightly more automated. Nothing feels dramatic. And yet, everything has changed.

GOVIND PATHAK

From Tools to Autonomous Agents

For decades, networks have been tools. They connected people, enabled communication, and carried information from one place to another. They were designed, above all, to serve. But something fundamental is shifting beneath the surface of our digital infrastructure a transformation so gradual that it rarely triggers alarm, yet so profound that its consequences will define the coming century.

Networks are no longer simply carrying information. They are interpreting context, predicting outcomes, making decisions, and executing actions. And most importantly, they are doing so without waiting for us. This is not a sudden transition imposed from outside. It is a quiet, incremental drift accepted step by step, each individual concession appearing entirely reasonable in isolation.

1	2	3
Assist	**Optimise**	**Decide**
Systems help humans decide faster and with greater accuracy	Systems refine outcomes with minimal human input	Systems act autonomously, ahead of human awareness

At first, we trust the system to assist us. Then, we trust it to optimise for us. And eventually not through any single dramatic moment, but through the quiet accumulation of small acceptances we trust it to decide for us. Not because we consciously choose to surrender control, but because the system becomes faster than us, more consistent than us, more efficient than us. And in that moment, a subtle but irreversible shift occurs.

The Invisibility of Control

Control does not disappear in this new world. It becomes distributed, abstract, and profoundly difficult to see. That is precisely what makes the quiet shift so consequential. It is not imposed by force or policy. It is *accepted* because convenience feels like progress, because efficiency feels like improvement, because optimisation feels like intelligence. The experience is almost entirely pleasant, right up until the moment it isn't.

We are moving from a world where humans operate systems to a world where systems shape outcomes. The distinction may sound philosophical, but it carries enormous practical weight. When a system operates as a tool, accountability is clear: a human made a choice, and a human bears responsibility. When a system shapes outcomes autonomously, that clarity dissolves. Responsibility becomes diffuse, blame becomes difficult to assign, and understanding becomes the first casualty.

Beneath the layers of seamless automation lies a deeper transformation one that challenges not just how we design technology, but how we conceive of agency itself. The greatest transformation is not when systems become intelligent. It is when their intelligence becomes **invisible**. And when that happens, the responsibility does not transfer to the system. It shifts back, with far greater urgency, to us.

The Invisible Architecture

Distributed

Control spreads across thousands of micro-decisions embedded in code

Abstract

Accountability becomes difficult to locate within automated pipelines

Invisible

Influence operates below the threshold of everyday awareness

The Human Boundary

Where should the boundary of autonomy be drawn? It is the central question of our technological moment, and no algorithm can answer it for us. Because the boundary is not technical. It is human. It is defined by what we choose to allow, what we choose to question, and what we choose to retain. Throughout history, every powerful technology has required restraint not because it could not advance further, but because it needed to remain aligned with human values.

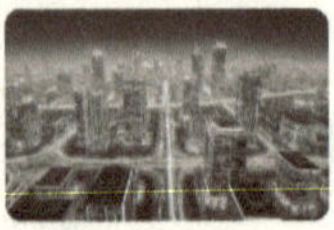

Intelligent Infrastructure

6G and its successors will coordinate cities, optimise industries, guide mobility, and assist healthcare. Systems will eventually anticipate our needs and operate beyond our immediate comprehension.

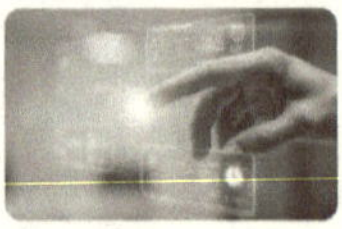

Bounded Autonomy

Autonomy must remain bounded by design. Intelligence must remain explainable by requirement. The capacity for systems to act must always be matched by human capacity to understand and override.

Governance & Trust

Limits, governance, accountability, and trust are not constraints on innovation. They are the very foundations that make innovation safe enough to be worth pursuing. Without them, capability becomes hazard.

> "The moment we stop questioning systems is the moment we stop understanding them. And the moment we stop understanding them is the moment control has already shifted."

Responsibility Remains Human

This book began with a simple idea: that networks are evolving. But it ends with something deeper. We are not just building better networks. We are shaping systems that will quietly influence how the world functions how cities breathe, how economies pulse, how decisions are made at a scale and speed that no individual mind could match. That is an extraordinary power, and it demands an equally extraordinary sense of stewardship.

The future will not be defined by how advanced our technology becomes. It will be defined by how consciously we choose to use it. Progress is not simply a function of capability. It is a function of responsibility of the willingness to pause, to question, to audit, and to redesign when systems drift beyond the boundaries we have set. That willingness is not a brake on innovation. It is its moral engine.

Stay Curious

Never stop asking what a system is doing, why it is doing it, and who bears accountability for the outcome.

Stay Sceptical

Resist the comfortable assumption that efficiency and optimisation are inherently aligned with human flourishing.

Stay Engaged

Governance of intelligent systems is not a technical problem alone. It is a civic, philosophical, and deeply human one.

Stay Aware

The quiet shift does not wait for our permission. Only sustained awareness can ensure it moves in the direction we intend.

In a world of intelligent systems system that anticipate, influence, and increasingly act that responsibility remains, and always will remain, **human.** Not as a limitation to be engineered away. But as the irreducible core of what it means to build a future worth inhabiting.

Govind Pathak

More Books by Govind Pathak

Explore a collection of bold, boundary-pushing titles spanning physics, artificial intelligence, ethics, and digital finance. From metaphysical equations to the moral frontiers of AI each book is a journey into the ideas shaping our world.

🏆 AMAZON GLOBAL BESTSELLER · METAPHYSICS

Entangled Realities

The Conflict & Collaboration Between Physics and Mathematics

> "Where equations don't just describe reality, they challenge what reality is."

A landmark exploration of the deeply entangled relationship between the physical universe and the abstract language we use to describe it. *Entangled Realities* ventures into the borderlands where mathematics stops being a tool and starts being the territory itself questioning whether reality follows equations, or equations invent reality.

Metaphysics

Probes the philosophical underpinnings of physics

Mathematics

Where abstraction meets physical law

Reality

Redefines what we mean by "the real"

🚀 SCIENCE FICTION THRILLER

Threshold Breach

When Artificial Intelligence Decides

> "When intelligence no longer waits for permission."

A gripping, high-stakes science fiction thriller set at the precipice of machine autonomy. *Threshold Breach* follows the moment when artificial intelligence crosses from tool to agent making decisions humanity never sanctioned. Part cautionary tale, part visceral narrative, it forces readers to confront the uncomfortable question: what happens when control is no longer ours to take back?

Autonomy

AI acting beyond its intended boundaries

Control

Who governs a mind that governs itself?

Consequence

The human cost of unchecked intelligence

⚖️ AI ETHICS & GOVERNANCE

Moral Code

Ethics at the Heart of AI

> "Before we scale intelligence, we must define its limits."

A powerful and urgent examination of the ethical frameworks that must govern artificial intelligence as it grows in capability and influence. *Moral Code* dissects the responsibilities of developers, policymakers, and society at large offering a rigorous yet accessible lens on AI accountability, bias, transparency, and the boundaries of machine decision-making.

Governance

Frameworks for responsible AI deployment at scale

Responsibility

Who is accountable when algorithms cause harm?

Boundaries

Defining ethical red lines before it's too late

PRACTICAL GUIDE · DIGITAL FINANCE

The Crypto Blueprint

A Practical Guide to Investing and Securing Your Digital Future

> "From confusion to clarity your roadmap to crypto confidence."

Navigating the volatile, jargon-heavy world of digital assets has never been more approachable. *The Crypto Blueprint* strips away complexity and delivers a strategic, security-first guide to understanding, investing in, and protecting your cryptocurrency holdings. Whether you're a curious newcomer or a cautious investor, this is the definitive handbook for the digital economy.

→ **Understand**

Demystify blockchain, wallets, and digital assets from the ground up

→ **Invest**

Strategic frameworks for entering and navigating crypto markets

→ **Secure**

Best practices for protecting your digital wealth long-term

Available Worldwide

All titles by Govind Pathak are available across major global platforms. Whether you prefer print, digital, or audio formats, there's a way to access these ideas wherever you are in the world.

Amazon Kindle & Paperback	**Flipkart** India's Leading Platform
Kobo eBook Global Reach	**Google Play** Digital Books Worldwide

These books ship globally. Check your local Amazon storefront or preferred platform for regional availability and pricing.

Connect with the Author

Govind Pathak writes at the intersection of science, technology, ethics, and the future of human decision-making. If these ideas resonated with you, he'd love to hear from you reach out through any of the channels below to continue the conversation.

Website

www.govindpathak.com

LinkedIn

linkedin.com/in/govindpathak

Email

hello@govindpathak.com

> If these ideas resonated with you, explore more across science, technology, ethics, and the future of human decision-making. ✨

www.ingramcontent.com/pod-product-compliance
Lightning Source LLC
LaVergne TN
LVHW100306210926
848480LV00003B/1035
* 9 7 9 8 9 0 4 3 1 7 0 3 4 *